Prai
Reinventin
Advice Profess...

A fascinating journey that reminds us just how much financial advice has changed over the past 40 years. Paul has been there throughout, and his insight creates a lively read that stirs many memories for those of us who were there and will leave those who weren't open-mouthed in disbelief.

Paul captures each phase of the market development with some fascinating interviews and uses his own experiences to draw telling conclusions and to provide a clear insight of how he sees the future of financial advice.

A labour of love, written with the same passion that Paul applies to his business.

— David Carrington

Paul presents a reflective and enjoyable canter of his experience in the distribution of financial planning advice during his long career. His experience through the window of recruitment reflects a broad and informed insight into how the industry has adapted to the challenges of regulation and is now evolving at pace into an emerging profession. He provides a helpful and informed insight into the fresh challenges of delivering financial planning advice in the digitised world.

— Derek Capelin

I would strongly recommend 'Reinventing the Financial Advice Profession' for anyone new to the industry, and for us old-timers! It is a great read and excellently portrays the evolution and changes in the financial services world over the last few decades.

It brought back so many happy memories, great people, great earnings and hard work with constant mergers and acquisitions!!

It's hard to believe where the industry has come from to where it is now, and this book excellently tells us that story.

— **John Hirst**

"If you can remember the sixties, you weren't there." is often quoted. Well, I was there and can also remember the seventies & eighties.

Looking back, it was, as Paul describes, a very different world. I started my FS career in 1968, like Paul also with L&G In the late seventies becoming a Building Society Inspector initially, as my first sales role also.

There were back then many expulsions from the Personal Investment Authority (PIA), the body that regulated retail financial services then. One very well-known company had a 700-strong sales army whose persistent 'smile and dial' selling techniques signed up 140,000 clients with £200m under management. The CEO used to burn £50 notes to motivate his commission-hungry sales team. Even the introduction of tighter regulations with the 1986 Financial Services Act made little difference at that time. Fortunately , times have now very much changed, for the good of the industry and more importantly the consumer.

Paul takes an earnest look back at what used to be and what was wrong with it and an insightful look forward for the possible future shape of the independent advisory world.

— **Peter Smith**

REINVENTING
— THE —
FINANCIAL
ADVICE
PROFESSION

FROM COMMISSION-DRIVEN SALESPEOPLE TO MULTI-MILLION POUND BUSINESSES

PAUL HARPER, MBA ACII Dip PFS

Cover image by: Wonderburg Creations
Book design by: SWATT Books Ltd

Printed in the United Kingdom
First Printing, 2022

ISBN: 978-1-7391293-0-9 (Paperback)
ISBN: 978-1-7391293-1-6 (eBook)

Paul Harper Publishing
Bristol BS39 4EU

www.paulharpersearch.co.uk

Contents

Acknowledgements

I started writing this book over lockdown as a personal challenge and something I have wanted to accomplish for many years. Little did I know quite how challenging writing a book would be.

I would like to thank everyone who contributed to the book, for your feedback and for your continued support.

I would also like to express my gratitude to my book mentor, Karen Williams, for all her support and guidance throughout this experience. Without you, this would not have been possible.

To my long-suffering team, who have supported me throughout the process, thank you and a special mention to Charlotte for keeping me on track when I lost the will!

And finally, I would like to thank my wife, Marie-Claire, who had to give up her dining room table for months. You gave me the courage to start writing this back in March 2020 and have always been my biggest cheerleader.

Foreword

I was intrigued when asked to provide a review for 'Reinventing the Financial Advice Profession' how Paul, as a subject matter expert of many years, had taken on his own challenge of approaching the book. Many books, and thought leadership articles and pieces, around the challenges and opportunities facing our industry can be frankly a bit dull, mundane and boring. I should have known that Paul, having decided to turn his hand to such a big project, would have found a way to make his reflections and observations thought-provoking, interesting, insightful and with more than a tinge of nostalgia back to his early days in and around the financial services industry. This helps to describe Paul as the individual, and now the author he is, by capturing the undoubted passion and enthusiasm he still has for people and what is now the financial services profession. This has helped Paul, as the book also clearly articulates, build up the resilience necessary continue to be successful in recruitment (and retention) and financial services, whilst also retaining his sense of humour and fun. His approach is infectious, and this comes across in spades.

To best understand where our industry is now and the significant progress for the better that has been made over the last 30+ years, a timeline I reluctantly now have to accept that I share myself, you have to understand where it came from. Reading Paul's own reflections helped to bring back many fond memories of my own, both in terms of how 'advice' was delivered and provided long before the days of RDR, but also some of my own old company cars, including a big white Peugeot 406 estate (which I actually loved) before moving on to a British racing green Ford Escort (which I loved even more). A bank provided free fuel card, which would be an absolute luxury in this day and age, also helped me to travel far and wide across the UK in the 1990's. Like Paul, I was very fortunate. However, I can also see why this needed to change.

On a more serious note, the book is one I would recommend to industry professionals both old(er) and young(er) as a great current reference point both for advisers and those such as myself in leadership positions, to better understand the challenges and opportunities we face now and those that lie ahead. Paul has set these out clearly in the closing chapters and has made a number of thought-provoking observations about the many different models and propositions, the pro's and con's of these different approaches, and how financial advice is now delivered, and also how it will continue to evolve further in the future. Whilst I didn't know Paul over 30 years ago, I feel as if I know him even better now, having had the opportunity to share his journey through the chapters and words he has crafted. I expect to refer back to the book again over the coming years as a future reference point too!

— **Iain Lightfoot**

Introduction

The 1980s were the glory days for financial advisers. The promise of flash cars, incentive trips and high commission cheques drove the profession. There were no barriers to entry. You could sell double glazing one week and be a financial adviser the following Monday.

Through to the 2000s, it was 'Sell! Sell! Sell!'. Although this was great for the commission-hungry financial adviser, it didn't give any longevity to the industry. In reality, a financial adviser's income was only as good as his or her last commission cheque, and the major focus was on winning new business rather than servicing and supporting existing clients.

During this time, the Financial Services Act started to change the profession, which led to an 89% decline in adviser numbers. Financial planning businesses had very little value. Most had self-employed advisers from whom the business skimmed off some commission and a percentage paid to brokers for introductions.

In reality, the industry had been in decline for 25 years, but it wasn't until 2013 that the tipping point happened. The Retail Distribution Review (RDR) led to a further drop of 25% of financial advisers in the three months after, as advisers saw the lost earning potential and chose not to take the qualifications required to continue.

The profession appeared to be on the edge of extinction. But it survived by a narrow squeak. It took a further 10 years for the industry to stabilise and start over again. And today, a typical small financial advice business could be valued in the £millions.

I believe that to be successful in UK financial planning you need to understand the history of the industry, the lessons learnt, and what you need to do differently. Rather than the commission culture of yesteryear, today, to build a thriving career and have business success requires you to focus on the client, embrace technology and have a credible people strategy.

Written for financial advisers, if you are new to the industry, my goal with this book is for you to realise that the industry hasn't always been as it is now and to see how the past has impacted what happens today.

If you've been in the business for decades, it will give you a great trip down memory lane, stir up some memories and you may well think "those were the days".

If you have picked up this book because you are a private equity partner or investor, you'll probably be saying to yourself "wasn't this terrible". And if you're a journalist or commentator, then you'll probably have suspected some of the stuff I share in these pages!

Using real-life examples from my 35+ years in the industry, with stories from others who have also lived through it, I explain what happened and why, how the market deteriorated and almost collapsed before its saviour arrived when least expected.

I start by delving into the history of financial services and its origins of the 'life assurance salesman', tracking the profession from its early Victorian beginnings through the 1960s era of the 'man from the Pru' into the 'Flash Harry' Unit-linked era, when commission was king, and conventions were lavish. Then I move through the bancassurance era and 'heyday' of the independent financial adviser (IFA) in the early 2000s to its near collapse in 2013.

Then I look at what happened next. How the market recovered, how the financial planning industry has evolved as a profession from the lifestyle-obsessed commission-hungry sales job to the professional client-focused role of today. Because today, financial advice business owners will find that even the very smallest IFA businesses have the potential to make the same owner a millionaire almost overnight.

I touch on the challenges the profession chases, and strategies for success. I don't tell you how to give financial advice. I provide an outline of how others have built and are building successful financial advice businesses, and what they can do differently in a post-pandemic world.

Let's face it, with only 27,000 financial advisers left, barriers to entry are high. The financial adviser today is usually oversubscribed, with more clients than he or she can handle. The cost of advice is the way most advisers ration their resource. Financial advisers are well remunerated, with typical total remuneration of around £100,000 per annum.

The position of a financial adviser is well respected and the businesses are starting to be profitable, even during the COVID-19 pandemic. This was noticed by investors in the City of London and elsewhere, as money has come flooding in. Since the pandemic, businesses are now focused on scaling and professionalising. The old guard are retiring or selling, and the new guard are inheriting businesses with stable income streams and demand exceeding supply.

In this book I explain how and why this has happened as well as attempting to address the question: Where do we go from here?

I'm not promising you all the answers, but this book gives you a fighting chance of succeeding.

About Paul Harper

If you're wondering who I am and why I'm qualified or experienced to talk about this topic, let me introduce myself. I am a financial services sales professional who has worked with financial advisers for over 35 years. Dip. PFS qualified, I also hold an MBA and am a Chartered Insurer.

I was born in the early 1960s and grew up in Bristol. It was an era when many large insurance companies were moving out of London, and several had relocated to Bristol. We had the head offices of Sun Life, Clerical Medical & General, Phoenix Life, London life and NatWest insurance services all employing hundreds of staff here.

I started work in 1981 at NatWest Insurance Services as a junior clerk in the commercial insurances department. Although it was a permanent job, I just took the job 'for the summer'. I intended to go to university, but my A level grades were lower than expected, so, rather than accept a less attractive course at a lesser university, I stayed.

My dad was a chartered banker and believed qualifications were the key to success. As an A level leaver, I was given a half-day release to go to night school to study for my ACII – something which my parents were keen for me to do.

I passed all three first year exams at first attempt, but I was getting frustrated by the lack of promotion opportunities – the company seemed to have a 'time served' culture.

While at night school I met a couple of lads who said they were becoming trainee life inspectors because they could be on the road with a company car in less than 12 months, which (as you'll find out later) was one of the reasons why the job appealed massively to me! When a trainee inspector job appeared at Legal & General, I applied and got it. Fortunately, the Life Branch Manager was ACII qualified and said he would support my exams, so I was able to make the move into life assurance but still keep my parents happy.

In 1983 I joined Legal & General and after one year at the Bristol Office, I was promoted to Life Inspector (nowadays that would be titled Business Development Manager) at the Cheltenham office. We were a market leader in low-cost endowments which were sold with mortgages. I called on insurance brokers but also on building societies. I had to collect green form leads from the building societies, I called their new borrowers and arranged to visit them in their homes.

Most appointments were in the evenings. I would meet with people, often young couples, who were taking out their first mortgage, explain the benefits of low-cost endowment mortgages over repayment mortgages, and persuade them to complete a proposal form. Most people signed and the building society received the commission, but I got a credit based on the annual premium equivalent, which went towards my target, and bonus.

At Legal & General I earned £6,000 basic and in my final year, bonuses took my total earnings to £8,800 plus a red company Vauxhall Cavalier.

L&G also relocated me to Cheltenham, gave me a subsidised mortgage and I bought my first flat at the age of 21. I liked the job but still yearned to return to Bristol. I never settled, and two years later, I moved back to Bristol to join Eagle Star Life as a Broker Consultant. Our products were really competitive, and I was given a good patch with some really good brokers to call on. There was no expectation for me to do evening calls.

I spent the next three years as a broker consultant, and they were some of the most enjoyable days of my life. I was back home with my friends but also doing a fabulous job which paid really well.

I started in the May of 1986. By the end of the first year, I was earning over £20,000 pa and rising fast. It was more than Dad's earnings as a bank manager, and I also had a company car.

However, it was all about sales success. Fortunately, I was successful and quickly made the top 5 sales list, qualifying for top performer conventions, and in 1989, when I was only 27 years old, I was promoted to Branch Manager in Northampton. The second youngest manager appointment at the time (I was one month older than a friend who was promoted on the same day).

I think it was fair to say no-one cared that I had passed my ACII around the same time. It was my sales success that mattered.

Looking back, the top point for the life assurance companies was around that time. We had 26 branches and 160 broker consultants. We were mid-sized compared to many of the large mutuals. Standard Life eventually peaked at around 350 broker consultants.

Once promoted to Branch Manager in Northampton, I went from strength to strength. We had a young team who were hungry for success. They built new broker relationships, secured new appointed representatives and rediscovered new ways of promoting old products, and sales flourished. When I took over the team it was in 23rd place out of 26 but by the end of the 1991 it was the top small branch and 11th overall. I qualified for the

Monte Carlo incentive trip with many of my team also attending. However, I hadn't realised that sales in many branches were declining.

We had a new Managing Director who was an actuary, and who decided to focus on cost cutting and building up our direct distribution which, for some bizarre reason, was seen as having more potential.

In a shock move, we closed half our branches and laid off the support staff. We separated IFA sales from direct distribution and appointed representatives – effectively creating two separate distribution channels with every branch having two different sales teams and management structures in it. We now know that this was not effective, but it was not so obvious at the time.

I took over the IFA sales team in Leicester, combining with the team in Northampton who, being top small branch, had just closed. I also had the strange task of taking over a team which consisted of the lowest and highest performing small branches in the UK. It felt like a betrayal for many of the team, seeing colleagues made redundant who had been seen as winners only a few months earlier.

12 months later, in 1994, the combined East Midlands team was top of the sales lists, and I was promoted to lead the flagship London region as Regional Manager. London was number 2 region at the time, so I had my sights set on being number 1.

Only 12 months later, the company announced it was closing all seven regional offices and downsizing to two regions and only 40 broker consultants. So, I attended our international cruise in September 1995 as top regional manager and the following month I was made redundant.

I was suddenly seeking a new job. Eagle Star had sponsored my MBA, and to be fair, they paid the balance of my fees. I completed the MBA and then became Sales Director of The Locum Group, a VCT-backed recruitment business which specialised in the supply of locum hospital doctors, GPs, supply teachers, ancillary medical professionals and social workers. It was an interesting profession but, while I helped the business secure participation in the NHS National framework, I don't think I was ideally suited to the high volume and activity but low skill aspects of the company.

Next, I tried my hand at headhunting, building the Bristol office of Hanover Search & Selection in 1998. I quickly grasped the key aspects of executive search and found my connections and experience to be invaluable.

In July 1999, I set up Paul Harper Search & Selection with my wife Marie-Claire and two employees.

22 years later I am still here. Today we specialise in all aspects of financial services, executive search, sourcing directors and specialists for financial services companies. This includes working on assignments to secure financial advisers for ambitious companies.

We also have a mergers and acquisitions business. We work with a small group of top financial services businesses, specialising in finding talent and acquisitions which will help them grow their business. For our key partners, we offer a variety of other services, from training to specialist recruitment.

With my experience, and the stories I share in this book, I truly believe that our past shapes the future. We now have new challenges to overcome, and these become easier to understand when we realise how and why the role has changed.

Interviews

Whilst writing this book, I had the opportunity to focus on the most important matters from my perspective, and I chose to interview people who'd been in their area of business for a while or who had specific interests in some of the matters I was covering.

When I started out, there were four key companies. Terry Ellis worked for two of them: the long-established safe and secure Prudential, then Abbey Life, in one of the first unit-linked life offices. Terry was an adviser who moved straight from selling clothes to selling insurance. He knew the commission era personally as well as the transition. He attended the sales conventions but remained as an adviser in the post commission era. He later worked for a couple of IFAs as compliance started to impact adviser sales and earnings.

I also interviewed Duncan Singer, who started off similarly to me as a Legal & General Broker Consultant calling on people in their homes to sell endowment mortgages, and also on brokers, the former name of IFAs. But, unlike me, Duncan chose to move to a mutual during the Campaign for Independent Financial Advice (CAMIFA) period, when IFAs decided to support those Life Offices who they perceived as supporting them. And like me, Duncan is still working in the industry today.

I spoke to Louise Hunt to gain an insight into Bancassurance, which was a key part of the industry for a short period. I chose Gillian Hepburn and Sharon Mattheus to talk about the industry's gender balance, or lack of it, what they see as the barriers to women and how these are now being addressed.

As the reward structure changed from commission to fees, the business model has started to change, but very few companies have yet adapted their approach to hiring. I interviewed Cameron Renton, a young financial adviser who has followed the traditional model. He backed himself, setting up as a self-employed independent financial adviser and is funding himself through the early years. It's hard but he has proven it can be done.

Then by contrast, I interviewed Benjamin Beck, a restricted financial adviser who has been fortunate enough to switch careers and train via an academy while working in employed paraplanner roles. His is a route most would prefer but is available to very few at present.

One of the consequences of the Retail Distribution Review (RDR) is the way that other professionals now work with financial planners. There was an exemption in the Financial Services Act for members of professional bodies, such as accountants, solicitors and insurance brokers to give financial advice using 'recognised professional body' (RPB) status. Even once that was lost, many were wary of financial advisers having access to their clients.

Today there is a new mutual respect between these professions. Dave Seager explained the unintended consequences of the Legal Service Act in this regard.

Finally, I was keen to understand the way companies are trying to attract and train the advisers of tomorrow. By speaking to Darren Smith, who effectively built out the Quilter Financial Adviser School after its acquisition, I was able to understand the challenges and early thinking. I then spoke to Julian Hince and Sean McKillop, who currently run the school, and the St James's Place Financial Adviser Academy. They explained the need to look wider than the academic training, and how both companies intend to ensure they can attract a wider base of candidates, not only second careerists but also graduates. They also talked about the challenges of bringing trainee advisers into a profession where self-employment is still a major block to people joining the industry.

You can find a more in-depth overview of the above-mentioned interviewees at the back of the book.

PART 1

The rise and fall

In my 40 years working with the financial adviser profession, I have seen many highs and lows in the profession that we now call financial advice and wealth management. But despite the changes, I believe it's in a better place than it has ever been. Whilst the COVID-19 lockdown will no doubt change the profession forever, it could have been so much worse.

When I started out, the profession was called Life Assurance – as in "he works in Life Assurance".

In theory, it's called Life 'Assurance' in the UK because pay-out is 'assured' as everyone dies eventually, whereas other forms of insurance only pay out in the event of an unlikely catastrophe. The Americans never understood this anyway and they called it 'Life Insurance' from day one!

In some cases, people used the title 'adviser' and even back in the late 1970s I saw terms such as 'investment adviser' start to be used, but there is no doubt that the profession was built on sales.

Ever since Mark Weinberg and Joel Joffe, who went on to found Abbey Life and Hambro Life, arrived in Britain allegedly wanting to find a way to sell stocks and shares door to door, there has been a movement to encourage the 'man and woman on the street' to not only protect his or her family in the event of death or loss, like the industrial insurance sales people of the 1950s and 1960s, but to start saving for his or her future through investment in the stock markets of the world.

In Part 1, I'll show you how it all started.

CHAPTER 1

Four direct sales companies

We can track innovation and progress back to four direct sales companies:

- Prudential
- Abbey Life
- Hambro Life (later called Allied Dunbar and Openwork)
- J Rothschild Assurance (later called St James's Place Partnership)

Prudential – Industrial Insurance

Prudential was the greatest of the UK Industrial Life Assurance companies, dating back to the start of the industrial era. I am a little too young to remember this era, but I understand that the man from the 'Pru' was an unassuming insurance man – and it was nearly always a man – who collected premiums weekly for insurance and savings plans to ensure people had protection for their possessions and life assurance. Initially they sold so-called 'penny policies' where a person could pay a penny a week in exchange for the promise of a lump sum on death which would cover the cost of their funeral expenses. This was a really important issue for society and Winston Churchill highlighted this in his speech on 26 October 1915.

"If I had my way, I would write the word 'insure' upon the door of every cottage and upon the blotting book of every public man, because I am convinced, for sacrifices so small, families and estates can be protected against catastrophes which would otherwise smash them up forever."

As they grew, traditional insurance companies also added savings plans which paid out after a given period, e.g. 10 years, or on a significant birthday, instead of on death. These 'with profits' plans had reversionary bonuses which could be added to a policy each year by the insurance company based on their profitability, and a terminal bonus that could be paid out when a policy matured. These first savings plans were well received but could only really have full value at maturity, so early surrenders had penalties and needed an actuary to calculate the surrender value.

Of course, the Prudential was not the only industrial insurance company. Other well-known players were Royal London, Royal Liver, Pearl Insurance, and Refuge Assurance.

Terry Ellis, now retired, worked in this era. As this was before my time, I asked him to share his experience in this chapter and how the industry progressed during this period. Terry started with Refuge Assurance before moving on to Pioneer Mutual, before eventually progressing to the most famous brand of all, the Prudential.

But it all started when he was working in retail clothes shop and told me how he was attracted to the Life Assurance industry. He told me:

"I met a friend who was working as an agent in Refuge Assurance. And he was earning about twice as much as me, so I wanted to find out more."

Terry went to meet his friend's dad, who was the Branch Manager and got the job.

"It was great because I had a good basic salary, and it was mainly selling IB – Industrial Branch (low premium policies paid weekly in cash where the insured person usually paid a small amount per month in exchange for a pay-out on death which would cover their funeral *costs) – and I used to get 4 x the premium as commission. So, if you sold something for £5 a month, you'd get £20 commission in return. When I was working in the clothes shop, I came out with about £29 a week, in my first week at the Refuge, I got £67. So, I thought – 'WOW!'"*

Around 1978, Terry made his first move to Pioneer Mutual to become an Industrial Business (IB) Representative, working with the agents to make sales.

"I outgrew my first agent job and I moved because I was quite ambitious then. I wanted to be a rep. as you got a company car, basic and commission. I went out with the agents to see customers in their homes, and it was quite an easy sale."

Terry's role was to upsell. He encouraged existing customers to increase their premiums and take out new policies as well as selling to other family members.

Terry enjoyed the agent's job at Pioneer Mutual. It was quite a prestigious job. His first company car was a mini and the agents gave him leads which he had to convert. When he was successful, both Terry and the agent received commission.

"It was quite nice because I used to just go off in my area, from Northampton to Luton and Bedford. A lot of these agents were ladies, and they were part time. They'd come with me and say, 'this is Terry, he has come to talk to you today'. So, it was my job to try and up the premium of the IB, which was quite easy to do really. Then I got commission, and they got commission – just for doing that."

Yes, it was all about the commission! Terry told me that the agents used to get 7 x the monthly premium and he received 3 x the increased monthly premium. Then, the Prudential came calling and he was offered a job with them in Northampton.

I asked him; apart from the money, why were the Prudential considered better than Refuge Assurance or Pioneer Mutual? Terry explained:

"People would buy from the Pru because of the name. The phrase the 'man from the Pru' started in the 1880s or 90s. It has been going for a very long time and was often used by people's parents and grandparents. They had always collected money from the door, so they were trusted. People were paid cash then, so they used to pay cash at the door, and pay-outs went to their children and their children's children."

Terry felt the Pru were a really good employer. He received a good basic salary plus commission. However, commission was not only paid for IB at 4 x the monthly premium; they also sold Ordinary Branch (OB) (policies paid by direct debit or standing order monthly from a bank account. They were for larger sums than IB policies), larger life assurance and savings plan premiums usually paid by direct debit. Finally, he earned commission on General Branch (GB) (general insurance, typically home and contents or car insurance which paid out on fire and theft or collision damage) sales because the Prudential offered a lot of general insurance products including car and house insurance.

Finally, there were other benefits.

"You got perks. I got a very cheap mortgage, something like 3% whereas at the time the mortgage rate was about 10%, and I used to get a car allowance, so I could choose my car up to about £2,000. I used to buy different cars, that's how it was then, I didn't have anything super flash, but it was a nice perk. I also got a non-contributory BUPA cover. I didn't pay anything. Yes, it was a really good job and I enjoyed doing it."

Abbey Life, established 1961 – Unit-linked

Abbey Life was set up in 1961 by Mark Weinberg. The famous unit-linked life assurance bond was legally sold as life assurance because it provided life assurance cover of 101% of the value of the bond on date of death. The investor purchased units in a fund, whose value reflected the underlying investments in the fund (mainly stocks and shares, property, and gilts).

The value of units could rise and fall but performed well in the long running bull market in that era. Unit-linked bonds were extremely popular, giving the average man or woman a chance to invest for significant returns. Of course, not all the health warnings were given in those days, and fortunes made were sometimes offset by fortunes lost.

Terry left his job at the Prudential to work in his family's garage business for a few years before joining Abbey Life as a self-employed adviser. He stayed for 15 years. He loved the sales culture, and he admired his manager who taught him how to increase sales and thus commission earnings.

> "He gave me an insight into working inside the direct salesforces in the commission-driven era.
>
> "The best thing about Abbey Life, for me, was that we had a really clever manager, and he had this very specific way of selling. Abbey Life used scripts, doing everything by script, getting referrals, getting appointments, the fact finding. We used to do loads of role plays, and I actually did very well there. They paid really good commissions and we also got some fantastic perks including conventions. I did quite well. I went to Florida and took my partner."

Abbey Life was extremely successful for many years before being purchased by Lloyds Bank to form Lloyds Abbey Life in 1988. Then it was absorbed into Lloyds Banking group in 1996 and closed to new business in 2000. During the early years it had the investment bond market mainly to itself while the stock market was performing exceptionally well, with the traditional insurance companies focusing on traditional life assurance and general insurance.

Hambro Life, 1970 (later known as Allied Dunbar), and the 'Unit-linked' era

Mark Weinberg, Lord Joffe and Sir Sidney Lipworth set up Hambro life in 1970 after Abbey Life was sold. Many of the early sales staff moved from Abbey Life.

It was known for its slick approach to sales in an era of light touch regulation. Like Abbey Life, sales staff were self-employed and rewarded by commission for selling new policies. Despite the stock market crash of 1974, pre-empted by the oil crisis, its clients benefited from the long bull run until 1987. This was the 'Unit-linked' era.

During this time, many of the traditional Life Offices copied Hambro Life and Abbey Life, setting up unit-linked offices to try to compete. Prudential set up Vanbrugh Life, General Accident set up The English Insurance Company, and many others followed – initially inventing new brands to hide behind.

Also, new overseas-based companies such as Skandia Life, Ambassador Life and Manulife entered the UK market in the unit-linked era, when the lack of requirement for a with-profits fund reduced barriers to entry. Eventually, Legal & General, Standard Life and Commercial Union all set up unit-linked companies using their own brands.

Hambro Life took minimum responsibility for its salesforce and became known for 'hard sell' tactics. The sales culture was embedded within all life assurance companies, but particularly the unit-linked direct sales companies from the 1970s to the 2000s and beyond.

Another bad trait was churning policies. As salespeople's main source of commission was to sell new business, there was a great temptation to persuade clients to cancel perfectly good policies and take out new ones.

An example of this would be an individual moving from one company to another and then encouraging their old clients to replace the policies they previously sold them, with policies from their new company. More about that later.

Eventually regulation was introduced in the form of the Financial Services Act 1986 which was designed to reduce the worst selling excesses of the unit-linked life assurance companies. The company was sold to British American Tobacco (BAT) and renamed Allied Dunbar. This was the time when I joined Eagle Star Life, part of Eagle Star Group, another company owned by BAT. However, whereas Eagle Star sold through IFAs, Allied Dunbar principally sold through its direct salesforce and had the not so affectionate nickname of "Allied Crowbar" due to its salesforce's reputation of 'force selling' to clients!

When the Financial Services Act started to bite, investigations of mis-selling followed. From 2001 to 2003, following a stock market fall, Allied Dunbar clients made many complaints, and even though some compensation was paid, the company was later fined by the FSA for mishandling complaints.

Later the business was sold to Zurich Life Group and after a couple of rebrands it became a stand-alone entity called Openwork, which is still trading today.

J Rothschild Assurance 1990 (later known as St James's Place Wealth Management)

At the end of the 1980s, Allied Dunbar (previously called Hambro Life) was purchased by British American Tobacco. After a major takeover battle, where Mark Weinberg and Jacob Rothschild (later Sir Mark Weinberg and Lord Rothschild), who were both on the BAT board at the time, unsuccessfully tried to take over BAT, the two industry heavy weights set up a new company called J Rothschild Assurance (JRA). This company is known today as St James's Place Wealth Management.

This followed on the previous formula of a self-employed salesforce (now called partners) and a highly sales-oriented culture (later dubbed 'Cufflinks and Cruises' by the press). Just like the previous time when advisers followed Mark Weinberg and Mike Wilson, his number 2, from Abbey Life to Hambro Life, they now followed them to J Rothschild Assurance.

I understand that the business's initial codename was Utopia Life which they designed to attract the top 20% of salespeople to the new company. It's fair to say they made the contract so attractive that the top salespeople would find it appealing, but it was all based on sales ability, not quality!

The other thing they made a big deal of was that they were a new company with no baggage regarding mis-selling which was big in 1992.

Unlike its predecessors, J Rothschild Assurance was not presented to the world as a life assurance company, but more as an investment company. The advisers were called partners and the offering was more sophisticated, still offering investment bonds but now offering a wide choice of funds and more than one fund manager. This situation was strengthened when depolarization was introduced in December 2004, which allowed the St James's Place partners to offer pensions and protection products from other leading companies.

Regulation was now much tighter, and initially commission disclosure, and later the Retail Distribution Review, meant the company (along with the other direct salesforces) had to overhaul its reward systems. However, the company focused on giving clients a full vertically integrated offering including adviser charges, product and platform charges, and investment management charges (often accused of being opaque).

However, it might be argued that the company's biggest single success was the way it overcame the threat of commission disclosure, and I will explore this further later. If anything, this company was even more successful than its predecessors, and went on to become the largest financial adviser/ Wealth Management business in the UK market, in terms of adviser numbers and client assets under advice. It has become a successful money-making business and in many ways its success and profitability has made it the financial advice business to which many other provider-owned adviser businesses aspire.

For most of this period leading up to 2012, the majority of financial advisers were 'salespeople', hunting clients first and advising second.

CHAPTER 1 SUMMARY

- Prudential was the largest direct sales company of the Victorian era and is still running today.

- Abbey Life established 1960 and the first unit-linked life assurance business.

- Hambro Life (later Allied Dunbar and now OpenWork) was established by management from Abbey Life when they left their original company.

- J Rothschild Assurance (now St James's Place), the third business established by the Abbey Life founders, was more focused on wealth management and called its self-employed advisers partners.

CHAPTER 2

The sales reward culture

Life assurance sales was very well paid in the 1980s and 1990s! When I received my first quarterly bonus at Eagle Star Life, I was 24. Suddenly I was earning more than my dad, who was a well-respected bank manager with over 25 years' banking experience and a chartered banker qualification.

The indemnity commission era supercharged life assurance sales from the mid-1970s to 2012. Although life assurance salespeople were already well rewarded, it went up a notch and the behaviours during this period were all driven by indemnity commission.

In the industrial insurance era, the general view was that life assurance is not bought, it has to be sold. So even the old industrial life sales staff from companies like Prudential, Pearl, Royal London, and Royal Liver were well rewarded and valued in their community.

It was a word-of-mouth era where life was hard; early death was common so pay-outs on death (even to cover funeral expenses) were appreciated. There was no equal pay, so women like my grandmother (who was widowed in 1938 when my dad was only 6 years old) earned much less than men.

As mentioned earlier, commission was paid to these financial advisers as a percentage of the annual premium, just the same as general insurance. Most people could understand this relationship but at some point, it changed.

During the 1970s, Equity and Law introduced indemnity commission for insurance brokers and agents. This meant capitalising the long tail of commission into an up-front lump sum. This might be 50% of the first year's premium on a savings plan, and over 100% on a life assurance policy.

From the mid-1970s to the end of 2012, most companies paid indemnity commission and it was the lifeblood of the market. Indemnity was a way of front-loading commissions on a policy – effectively paying it in advance. Rather than pay a relatively small amount of commission every year throughout the life of a policy, indemnity commission assumed a policy would run for its full term (often 25 years) and paid the financial adviser almost the whole amount in one go, as soon as the policy went 'on risk'.

Terry Ellis told me:

> "If you sold an average Pensions scheme for about £25 a month, you would get something back like £200 commission".

Of course, these fees were deducted from the client's product via charges using a variety of opaque, clever structures. It seems unlikely that the average consumer understood just how much commission the adviser was receiving on a policy with a relatively small monthly premium.

The most popular way to do this initially was by use of a non-allocation period (not adding any value to a client's investments for a period). Another method was to have initial units – making heavy charges on the first two years' investments and bid/offer spreads (further reducing the value of any investment by 5–7%).

As these were gradually outlawed, the preferred method became early surrender charges. This allowed companies to give the impression the customer did not face an initial charge, but the early surrender charge achieved the same thing by ensuring all customers paid the full charge, either over the life of the policy or on early surrender.

During the unit-linked era (Abbey life, Hambro Life, and J Rothschild Assurance) the major motivation tool used by most life assurance companies was indemnity commission.

Initially that meant most investment products for the masses were sold by company salesforces, whereas the rich remained with their stockbrokers (Charles Stanley was set up in 1792).

Terry Ellis again talks about the sales culture at Abbey Life:

> "The beautiful thing then was when I first started you didn't even have a fact-find, you could just sell to anybody. One guy I knew used to sell to the taxi drivers and shopkeepers, and anywhere in London, wherever we went, he would just sell, and all we had to do then was to get a little signature, give your bank details and that was that. So, 'if you had the balls, you got the goods.'

> "The people were quite flash at Abbey Life – I did quite well, but some of them came from London; they were earning hundreds of thousands of pounds a year, and that was a lot of money in the mid-1980s!"

With virtually no cost for training or regulation, and a commission-only salesforce, the direct sales companies grew by hiring more and more financial advisers.

Many companies competed on the amount of commission paid to salespeople, be they direct salespeople or brokers; so, in an era when charges were opaque and commissions were not disclosed, the charging structures favoured the advisers over the clients.

> As Terry outlined to me: "The Abbey Life cover master policy had life cover and savings incorporated in it. As a very long-term policy, it paid very good commission. For £15 a month premium it gave me £200. That's higher than pensions and also higher than the total a customer paid in the first year, because the longer the term, the higher the commission."

Later in his career, Terry became an IFA and had to disclose commission to his clients, which he found difficult to do, but he said customers in the 1980s and 1990s rarely asked how much commission he earned.

Looking back, commission was the lifeblood that funded the lifestyles of those who built the industry, but it had two problems:

1. It was transactional – so people only got paid when new business was sold;
2. It was not equal across the product providers or their range of products.

So, brokers and IFAs could be paid different amounts by different companies. No wonder it became a battleground. Commission levels could influence salespeople's behaviours – and the consumer would never know!

Incentive Schemes, Company Conventions and other Perks

As well as commission, the providers used other methods to reward their best life assurance salespeople.

The first was the 'override commission' – a higher amount payable to the top salespeople (presumably to recognise economies of scale). Of course, these rewards also acted as a retention tool. Other popular tools were sales competitions, company cars and overseas conventions.

When I was young, we used to hear stories from the USA of top salespeople being handed wads of cash (sometimes thousands of dollars) at a team meeting. I never witnessed that in the UK, but I can certainly remember a colleague of mine at Legal & General being awarded a gold watch for winning a sales competition and I certainly won designer luggage and many all-expenses paid trips to London and elsewhere, with a West End show and a stay with my partner in a top London hotel.

The greatest prize of them all was the overseas company convention. While they are frowned upon now, I must confess I have benefitted from these incentives in the past.

In my time working for Eagle Star Life, I qualified for three incentive trips:

*   Bangkok;
*   Monte Carlo;
*   Mediterranean cruise – on the 'Silver Cloud'.

I can truly say that we were treated truly magnificently on all three, and they certainly incentivised me to achieve the extra sales necessary.

What I really loved about Eagle Star Life was that we were part of a global company, and the overseas conventions were not just for top UK performers but also for our Eagle Star International Life counterparts from all over the World, including delegates from Australia, Dubai, Hong Kong, France, Spain, Italy and South America. Surprisingly perhaps to our UK thinking, many of the overseas delegates also brought their top brokers with them.

Those who qualified attended with their partners, and there were hundreds of us from across the world. No expense was spared, and of course, it wasn't uncommon for foreign countries to compete for incentive trips.

When we went to Thailand with Eagle Star Life, I was told that we were the largest company conference to have been held in Bangkok at that stage. As a result, the Crown Prince of Thailand attended one of our banquets. We had many fabulous trips as well as a private concert with Grace Kennedy. I remember the five-star hotel, the Ice Sculptures, the elephant in the ballroom – yes really! He could take cash and peanuts from us with his trunk. He ate the peanuts and put the cash in his handler's pocket! An act that would be definitely frowned upon now.

In the next few years, many other companies took their teams to Thailand, and I am sure that they too had a magnificent time.

In Monte Carlo, which was an Eagle Star UK convention, I recall we stayed at the Hotel Hermitage on the square. Impressive, but not quite as lavish as Bangkok.

Fortunately, my last convention with Eagle Star topped them all. This was the Eagle Star International Life Convention in 1995. The UK delegates and partners were flown out to Barcelona where we boarded the 'Silver Cloud', a 6-star cruise ship which took us on a Mediterranean cruise, and it really was out of this world. We were told that all food and drink including room service was free (including normal champagne but not vintage). We had world class performers and magicians on the Cruise liner. The boat had twice as many crew as the number of guests and the service and entertainment were superb. Entertainers flew out to the ship to perform, and we stopped in Florence, Monte Carlo and Palma. By that stage I was a Regional Manager attending, so my wife and I were given a superior room with a balcony.

Terry Ellis also enjoyed an Abbey Life Convention in Florida with his partner. He told me that Abbey Life sent around 3,000 delegates. Unlike Eagle Star Life, which had a relatively small broker sales team, Abbey Life, which had a very large direct sales team, had different levels of convention. The top one was the Chairman's club. They earned £100,000 plus and had a special green jacket.

> "There was a story actually that the Chairman's club, the elite salesmen went to Iran. Some of our top salespeople, including our 'Chief Consultant' were by the swimming pool and they decided to phone up the Shah of Iran and they eventually got through to him, and wanted to talk to him about investments. I think the Shah met him, because he was our chief and he did buy some investments. You know, you got to try, and sometimes you succeed!"

Not surprisingly, once you attended one convention, you wanted to go every year. I told my colleagues back home the stories and they wanted to attend the next one.

Originally, companies claimed conventions as an expense. Later rules became stricter, and it became necessary for conventions to have a few 'notional' business sessions.

I recall one session about a specialist policy we were launching and one which equated lion behaviour to human behaviour. However, the giveaway was that only the top sales performers (and their partners) were invited. Advisers would compete all year for the chance to attend and winning was everything.

The working session might involve special guests. At my first convention, the highlight of the whole trip was to meet Neil Armstrong, the first man on the Moon. Using 'The Eagle Has Landed' as our theme, the organisers blended Eagle Star with 'the Eagle' landing craft on Apollo 11 to create a narrative for the convention.

He spoke about the importance of teamwork in ensuring the USA beat the Soviet Union in its quest to get the first man on the moon. I'm not sure whether it taught us anything, but it was a fabulous experience. As one of the top UK performers, I enjoyed a drink with him at the bar the night before his speech. It was truly special.

Of course, as a Broker Consultant and later a Manager, I was once removed from the advice process. While my company could incentivise me, my aim was to persuade an IFA to recommend our products. I couldn't actually direct a client to use us, and while some of the smaller companies took brokers on overseas convention, we never could. The biggest incentive I was allowed to offer was to take a broker to lunch (or to corporate entertainment such as Cheltenham races!).

Direct Sales companies were most associated with offering a multitude of incentives and overseas conventions. They directly persuaded clients to purchase their products.

As HMRC began to bite back by taxing company incentive trips, companies initially covered the additional tax cost but the PAYE system in the UK caused tax issues because some people objected when they were charged 'Benefit in Kind' on prizes they said they didn't really want and started requesting cash equivalents instead.

Not just direct sales companies

Finally, I can't ignore the fact that IFA Groups also ran overseas conventions for their members, and these were, at least partly, funded by life assurance companies and other product providers. Many of the larger networks received 'marketing allowances' from product providers and, as any self-respecting National Account Manager will admit, the marketing allowance gave them influence and 'permission to play'. It gave the provider access to the membership of an IFA network including the opportunity to present at national conferences and roadshows, inclusion on Best Advice panels, management information about individual member companies and plenty of other opportunities to influence the membership.

A few years ago, many IFA Networks held overseas conferences for their members (on a much lower budget than the ones I described above) and funded by the providers, but this gradually died out and certainly the Networks have been keen to distance themselves from provider funding since 2013.

Although most companies cut back on incentive trips for cost reasons many years ago, the higher charging direct salesforces kept going until much more recently.

Even until quite recently St James's Place offered a range of conventions to its most successful partners. The top sales people often attended more than one in a year and I have no doubt they were as lavish and motivational as those I attended.

In fact, St James's Place only ceased its overseas conventions in 2019 following heavy criticism in the press for its 'Cruises and Cufflinks' culture.

Today, we still see bonus schemes but no longer see the other incentive schemes. While some may rue the end of these incentives, it must be right for the client and it's hard to believe that the opportunity to attend an all-expenses paid free trip with your partner to some exotic location wouldn't influence you at all.

Cars and other benefits

When I was growing up, I had dreams of getting a job with a company car. As I mentioned earlier, you could say that this is why I got into Life Assurance sales. My dad had a respectable job at a bank and my family expected me to follow the same route. But my dad had a beaten-up Ford Cortina Estate!

There was a man at the end of the road who had a brand-new Ford Capri; the car that I aspired to drive. I found out that this man was a sales rep, and the Capri was his company car.

But my parents wanted me to get a good job and pass my professional exams. Being a sales rep was not a path they wanted me to follow. Yet I wanted to find out how I could get a car like this.

I started my career working within the insurance broker division of NatWest bank. The senior managers had company cars, but it quickly became apparent to me that promotion in a bank at that time was largely based on time served. The idea of waiting 10 years to get a company car didn't appeal to me.

I probably would have stayed there if it wasn't for a friend of mine moving to an insurance company as a trainee inspector. He explained that he could carry on taking his professional exams, but within a year he might well be out on the road with a company car. You can imagine my excitement. I could meet my parents' expectations by continuing with my professional examinations but also get a job with a company car.

Within three months, I too had secured a job as a trainee inspector with Legal & General and, to be fair to them, within a year I was out on the road with my car. It wasn't quite the Ford Capri I aspired to drive. Instead, as a trainee I was given a couple of pool cars when running errands for the other inspectors. I was firstly given a fluorescent green Morris Ital which was left to me by my predecessor. I was told that he'd ordered it while drunk and regretted it from the day he had it. It was a truly terrible car with a gearbox as fierce as a lion which often led to squealing the clutch as it bunny hopped down the road.

Shortly after that, I was given a second-hand Vauxhall Cavalier. It was a 1.2 base model, but a Cavalier was an aspirational car, and I was delighted to have it.

Finally, I was allowed to order my first brand new company car of my choice. I had a 1.3 litre base model Vauxhall Cavalier in bright red, which I loved! Most of my colleagues also had the same, but the two senior consultants had Vauxhall Cavalier GL model, and the manager had an Austin Montego, a similar size to a five series BMW today. At that time the main topic of conversation in the office was company cars.

Status was really important. Over the next few years, I traded up from base level Vauxhall cavaliers Ls and GLs. In those days, we had to have British made cars, and this meant one of four brands:

- Ford;
- Vauxhall;
- Rover;
- Chrysler.

We all thought Chryslers were 'rubbish' and at Legal & General the discerning choice for most of us was a Vauxhall Cavalier. When I moved to Eagle Star, I got a Ford Escort which had a 1.4 litre Lean Burn engine.

The other important thing in the company car was the quality of stereo you had. We'd start off with just a radio and progressed to a radio cassette with stereo speakers. It was the bee's knees!

Then the Anglo-American Chrysler was purchased by Peugeot, which meant that our consultants could also have Peugeots, Renaults and Citroens.

When I moved up to Manager, the first car I got was a metallic blue Peugeot 405 Sri. It was a fantastic car. It had first appeared in television adverts being driven through forest fires with 'Take my Breath Away', the theme to *Top Gun*, being played in the background.

Generally, my team of broker consultants went through fads. They tended to choose whichever car was most popular at the time, so there were various periods when people chose Escorts or Astras, Citroen Xantias or Rovers. Back in the day, Rovers carried quite a lot of prestige, but they gradually became less and less reliable.

This was a stage in my life when I had several car accidents and wrote off a couple of cars, so I worked my way through a series of Renaults, Peugeots and Volkswagens before the company's car scheme changed the game.

I mentioned before that we had to have British made (and later some EU made) cars. However, in my earlier years, the car you could have was purchased by your company and therefore the choice of cars was usually based on retail price. Occasionally it would be possible to get a more highly priced car if it was on discount. An example was the Alfa Romeo T Spark.

I remember at one time the company was able to get this car quite cheaply and suddenly most of the managers around me were getting them. The problem the company had was that the resale value on the Alfa (which tended to fall apart) was extremely low, so while it may have suited the prestige of the managers, it was probably financially damaging for the company.

Then in 1994, many companies changed from car purchase to car lease and the difference was amazing. Suddenly, it was not the retail price which mattered but the overall cost of ownership including depreciation. Suddenly, cars with good depreciation values such as BMWs and Mercedes came into our target range. I remember when I first got my first C-Class Mercedes and within short time so did all my colleagues. We really thought we had hit the big time then.

Nowadays it's hard to remember that companies had a very restrictive range of cars and that the sign of success would be a Ford Granada or Rover 800, whereas now, in the age of car allowances and freedom, it's almost obligatory for a senior manager to have a big German car such as a 5 Series BMW, an E Class Mercedes, or an Audi A6 or its English equivalent; and my personal favourites, the Jaguar XF or F-Pace, although, of course, the electric cars are gaining traction and anything goes. I even looked at an electric Jaguar I-Pace recently before deciding it is just too expensive to justify at present!

Using Car Schemes and Incentives to Recruit and Retain

Companies generally used car schemes and incentives to recruit and retain staff, and I nearly didn't move from to Legal & General to Eagle Star because the company car scheme was not as good.

At Legal & General I had a new red Vauxhall Cavalier whereas Eagle Star only offered Vauxhall Astras and Ford Escorts. In the end, the chance to have a basic salary of £10,500pa – which was significantly above my basic earnings at L&G of £6,600pa, with total earnings, including a bonus of £8,800 – and the chance to move back to Bristol from Cheltenham, persuaded me, but I do remember the embarrassment of having to drive up to see my friends in an 'inferior' car. However, when I started earning more than my dad, the embarrassment of a car didn't seem so bad!

After redundancy and a couple of years away from financial services, I returned on the executive search side, still working with financial services companies. When I set up my company in 1999, I was able to use my knowledge of company cars.

Back in the early 2000s my company was retained to build the sales team for a relative newcomer to the UK market. The company was called Winterthur Life. It offered a specialist range of self-invested personal pensions (SIPPs) but was relatively small compared to its competitors. We knew that we needed an edge to hire consultants for this relatively unknown company, and, would you believe, we used the company car.

Whereas most companies offered brand new but a fairly boring choice of company cars, Winterthur offered consultants a more prestigious choice of company car, albeit around 12 months old. This car scheme probably cost less than its competitors, because they could buy older cars, but had the advantage of being more flexible.

When we were headhunting for consultants from their competitors, we were able to use this to our advantage. By buying cars a year older, business development managers (BDMs) could afford such prestige cars as Rover 600s and 800s, or convertibles and 'people carriers', which were frowned on by other companies at the time. We and the Winterthur Hiring Managers were able to use this as a selling point, making out that a Winterthur BDM role was more prestigious than with other companies.

It really worked and we secured some of the best BDMs in the market for them from their competitors. Eventually they won the prestigious sales team of the year at a major industry awards ceremony.

Company cars and other incentives provided a great recruitment tool for skilled managers and head-hunters.

Company cars in the future

Of course, company cars have now gone out of fashion. However, within many companies there is a car allowance and sometimes some form of car scheme. It is much less common in Wealth Management and the IFA world, but until COVID hit, most company BDMs still received some sort of car allowance as well as being able to claim back a mileage allowance. That's the problem with Government tax schemes, there's always some way around it!

We don't know what the future will hold, but on a zoom conference recently, half the IFAs seemed to have Teslas. Maybe we will all move to electric cars next, particularly as the prices drop, but I think it's likely that many people will be actively wondering if it's sensible to be spending a lot of their hard-earned income or car allowance on cars.

Maybe, with Uber driverless cars just around the corner and the likelihood of travelling much less, we've finally seen the total demise of the company car for all but the chauffer-driven executives!

In recent years, the financial advice profession has failed to attract new blood at the same rate as people leave. So, while company cars, incentives and commissions of the past undoubtedly attracted many of us to the profession, it appears we have not yet found a way to attract the next generation in the way we might like.

CHAPTER 2 SUMMARY

- Indemnity commission supercharged life assurance sales from the mid-1970s to 2012.

- High commission and no perceivable barriers to entry created a sales culture.

- Indemnity commission encouraged some poor sales practices.

- It was transactional so replacing one product with another generated new commission.

- Commission payments were not equal across all product providers.

- The company car was given as a perk. The type of car displayed the level of an individual's sales success.

- Companies provided additional incentives such as overseas holidays to encourage sales.

- Not just direct sales companies – many IFAs used the same approach.

CHAPTER 3

The rise of the Insurance Intermediary

When I entered the market as a young 'Life Inspector' there were a lot of companies and a lot of different ways to distribute. The direct salesforces were still going strong with smart young people (mainly men) in sharp suits and flash cars, but I didn't deal with them.

Although direct sales was the dominant distribution channel for life assurance and investment products through the 1970s, 1980s and early 1990s, a combination of legislation and the big traditional companies trying to dominate the sector led to more emphasis on intermediated sales.

From early on, insurance agents and insurance brokers offered life assurance and pensions advice. In fact, many also acted as building society agencies and estate agencies, taking savings plan payments and investment deposits as well. With this already in place, it's not surprising they added life assurance savings plans, but their more passive, 'service-based' sale struggled to compete with the optimistic, more salesy approach of the direct salesperson.

Once the major direct sales companies such as Abbey Life and Hambro Life gained traction with unit-linked products, it's not surprising that they looked to distribute their products via insurance brokers and agents as well as via their own salesforces.

The insurance brokers and agents were selling life assurance alongside general insurance. Usually, they had agencies with the traditional large general insurance companies such as Prudential, Legal & General, GRE, Royal, Sun Alliance (later merged to become Royal Sun Alliance), Norwich Union, Commercial Union and General Accident (who also later merged), but also the traditional life assurance companies.

At that stage, the traditional companies were dominated by Scottish-based mutual companies who were owned by their policyholders, such as Standard Life, Scottish Life, Scottish Mutual, Scottish Equitable, Scottish Widows and Scottish Amicable. Apparently, we all felt the Scots were good with money!

As a Life Inspector for Legal & General in 1984, I had two types of customers:

1. The insurance brokers and agents;
2. The Building Society Managers.

The building societies were selling endowment policies as a means of mortgage repayment.

Most building societies had a partnership with one of the big traditional insurers. For instance, at Legal & General we were partnered with the Woolwich and Abbey National. Sun Alliance was partnered with the Halifax and GRE were partnered with Nationwide. When I moved from Legal & General to Eagle Star Life, my new employer's biggest partnership was with Bradford & Bingley Building Society.

These building societies received commission for selling the products and, in many ways, this might be what led to the creation of the Bancassurance sector many years later. The customers, of course, had no way of fully understanding all this. If they went to the building society for a mortgage, they might have been told that they had to take an endowment alongside, or they might have been given the option and commission may or may not have been mentioned.

The concept of an endowment mortgage was that the customer took out an endowment policy which not only provided life assurance cover but also was part savings plan, and was designed to pay out a lump sum at maturity which would be more than equal to the value of the mortgage, hopefully resulting in an additional lump sum as well. The mortgage buyer paid interest only on the mortgage, so costs were very similar to a traditional repayment mortgage with the likely benefit of an additional pay-out after the mortgage was repaid.

Of course, it did rely on a level of investment return which was feasible in a high inflationary climate but less likely in the lower inflationary climate we have seen in recent years. In theory, as mortgage payments reduced, people should have saved more but that was rarely mentioned.

Working at Legal & General at that time, the building society manager didn't even have to make the sale, I did it for him or her. The manager gave me a green form (so called due to its colour); I then rang the customer and offered to visit him, her or them at home to explain the options to them; and he, she or they nearly always accepted the offer.

Duncan Singer is now a Divisional Manager for the Savings & Retirement business at Aviva, but back in the late 1980s, he started off as a Life Inspector, like me, at Legal & General. This is what he said about the era:

> "Prior to the Financial Services Act 1986 it was perfectly OK for Life Inspectors to discuss mortgage repayment methods directly with clients on behalf of the building societies who were lending the money. So, developing strong relationships with local Building Society Managers was key to being a successful Life Inspector back in those days, as the Building Society were directly remunerated by the Life Company for any life assurance or mortgage repayment products that were 'sold' to these clients, usually by a lump sum payment called an indemnity commission. There was strong competition for these leads amongst the numerous Life Companies that existed at that time. The business arrangement was also reciprocal with some of the Building Societies where we would introduce referred clients to the Building Societies from Mortgage Brokers."

Over the years this changed, and later on it was the estate agencies who pre-sold the endowment mortgages to customers.

Insurance agents and brokers

To sell insurance, you needed an agency with an insurance company, and they would pay you for selling their product. As a young inspector, one of my tasks was to 'inspect' potential new agents and decide whether they could have an agency with us, and if so, whether they could receive indemnity commission. My understanding was that this depended on ensuring the agent would keep the business on the books during the commission clawback period and, if it not, that they would be able to pay us back. We tended to look at lapse rates and financial probity. We knew that if we refused indemnity payments we wouldn't receive any business from that agent, so there was tension between sales, who would willingly grant indemnity terms to all agents, and finance, who sometimes refused.

While most people understood there was a commission payment made by the life assurance company to the salesperson, I mentioned before that the amount was not disclosed and for many it was really difficult to tell a life assurance salesman from a broker or independent adviser. Even the direct salesperson often had several agencies with life companies. They tended to give the impression of independence while still favouring their main company.

As a result of the vast amounts now payable to people selling life assurance, the market grew, and fortunes were earned. In bull markets (1974 to 1987), customers, financial salespeople and advisers all made money, but that was about to change.

Legislation and tax relief

Life Assurance Premium Relief (LAPR)

It could be reasonably argued that changes in legislation have always driven the financial services profession, but perhaps the most important government tax break was that which was granted in the early days of life insurance.

From as early as I can remember, everyone told me that life insurance received premium relief, known as Life Assurance Premium Relief (LAPR). It meant that half the basic rate of tax (17.5%) was deducted from each premium and paid by the government. It was the backbone of a life assurance salesman's armoury as you could say that the government wanted you to save, wanted you to pay for life insurance to protect your family. And who can resist a government tax break?

In fact, this was probably the reason why Joel Joffe and Mark Weinberg felt that life insurance was the appropriate vehicle to use to sell stocks and shares when they first came to England and set up Abbey Life in 1960.

So, a 17.5% saving on a savings plan would have made it even more attractive as it was just the government giving you back your own money and increased the speed of growth of your savings.

Unfortunately for me, this all came to end in March 1984, when Nigel Lawson, the Chancellor of the Exchequer stated that as at midnight that night (13 March 1984) he was ending LAPR and there would be no more tax relief on life insurance.

I had only recently started at Legal & General, and we had a manic few hours as every life insurance policy application in the Bristol branch where I worked, had to be registered and sent to the head office to go on risk by midnight. I remember all sorts of shenanigans. There were cases where clients wanted the policy but couldn't get to us. There were cases where brokers wanted policies to put on risk without the client's explicit permission. We had some weird and wonderful cases. I was a young insurance clerk at the time, but I can remember some of the inspectors holding forms up to the window to copy customers' signatures onto direct debit mandates, and other dodgy practices.

What I also remember then was that many people were predicting the end of the life assurance industry, which was a bit of a problem for me as I'd only recently entered it.

Nevertheless, the industry adapted, and very quickly the benefit of LAPR was forgotten and other benefits of savings investments on life insurance were promoted.

Mortgage Interest Relief at Source (MIRAS)

One of the benefits of having a mortgage back in those days was that people received Mortgage Interest Relief at Source on the first £30,000 of their mortgage. When the average mortgage probably wasn't much more than this, this was extremely attractive.

My first flat in Cheltenham cost £21,250 in 1984 and my first house when I returned to Bristol (a three-bedroom semi-detached) only cost £35,000 in 1986.

During the late 1980s, as house prices rose, we had an anomaly in the system which meant that married couples were only entitled to one MIRAS amount, i.e. £30,000, whereas unmarried couples (which was increasingly becoming more common) could claim double MIRAS, as each of the individuals was entitled to £30,000.

During the late '80s there was a housing sale boom as young couples piled into a rising market. This double MIRAS ended on the 30th of June 1988, and particularly in the later days running up to the deadline there was a clamour for people to complete on their mortgages. Unfortunately, once double MIRAS ended we saw a housing market collapse.

I bought my next house (a four-bed detached) in March 1988 for £83,000. And having spent a lot of money on improving it, I sold it for £77,000 two years later. When I bought my house, the area was called Bradley Stoke; when I left, it was widely known by the nickname 'Sadly Broke'!

I was fortunate. As Eagle Star was relocating me to Northampton, they bailed me out by covering the negative equity on my next house, but others weren't so fortunate, and the housing market was stagnant for a very long time. I lost even more money on my next house. Buying at £120,000 in 1990 and selling at £97,000 in 1993. And I remember a colleague of mine at Eagle Star who bought a brand new house for £120,000 in 1989 and sold it for around £80,000 when they were relocated only a couple of years later.

It could probably be argued that this was the heyday of endowment policies, which led to a mass of complaints in the late 1990s and early

2000s when a stock market drop led to a reduction in pay-outs, which didn't necessarily cover people's expectations (or their mortgages).

Light touch regulation – the Financial Services Act 1986

Until 1987 there were no barriers to entry in the finance industry. There was no minimum qualification, and anyone could call him or herself a financial adviser in the UK or indeed, most countries in the World, but potential rewards were high for any 'would be' salesperson. So, high rewards and low barriers... What could possibly go wrong?!

From 1987, when the Financial Services Act (1986) was introduced, regulation started the long move towards professionalisation.

Firstly, the market became self-regulated; and secondly, the way financial advice was delivered and the responsibility which went with that moved the market from the legal concept of 'caveat emptor' (buyer beware) to financial advisers and their companies being held responsible for the advice they gave to clients, as consumer protection laws were introduced.

The act introduced a lot of new concepts for financial advice. The most important were that all financial advisers needed a basic level of qualification. This was the Financial Planning Certificate (FPC). By today's standards it was extremely low level. It was two multiple choice papers (FP1 and FP2), and a slightly more detailed paper (FP3).

Terry Ellis told me:

> "Before I left Abbey Life, we all had to take the exams.We had to do the FPC levels 1 2 3, and then there were various other exams started creeping in. Abbey Life was geared to learning and going over everything, so the exams weren't too difficult."

It did, however, prevent certain people working in the industry who (it could be argued) should never have been there in the first place. Back in those days I recall a milkman who was a registered agent with my company. He was given an agency by the company at some time in the past and produced a reasonable amount of new business. The introduction of the Financial Services Act, and the accompanying minimum examination requirement caused him to cease giving financial advice, but he could still act as an introducer. He became a tied agent of our company and continued introducing business to one of our financial consultants.

Polarisation and the rise of the Independent Financial Adviser

During the following few years, there was a significant change in the balance between direct salesforces and IFAs. The once all-powerful direct salesforces certainly lost out significantly during this period. One of the very significant reasons for this was polarisation.

Polarisation rules stated that an adviser was either independent or tied. A tied agent (officially called an appointed representative) could only sell the products of one company. That meant they often did not have a full range of products to present to their customers. Even if they had a full product range, they often found that some of these products were not competitive. This had a massive impact on the industry as it had the effect of disadvantaging direct salespeople (which was probably the intention).

A major issue for direct sales companies was that companies did not always offer a full range of products and so suitable advice meant selling the most suitable product from its range. I recall many direct salesforces did not have permanent health insurance (PHI) products, so taught their sales teams to sell critical illness as the closest alternative. It had the advantage of being cheaper and easier to underwrite (so faster to get on the books and get paid commission) but critical illness was not really a directly comparable product. I suspect that sales of PHI dropped off in this period – not the intention when the legislation was passed, I'm sure!

A direct salesperson would often have a good trusting relationship with a client who needed life assurance. They would initially request and receive a quotation by their trusted adviser, but they then might receive a recommendation from someone else that they could do it far cheaper through an IFA.

IFAs, by having coverage of the whole market could usually get much cheaper life assurance than the tied agent or the direct salesperson. That would then have a tendency to break the bond of trust and in many cases the IFA would win the client. During this period there was a lot of conflict between companies.

In order to avoid their salespeople losing clients to IFAs, some large companies attempted to circumnavigate the rules by having an independent advice arm which could be used, this wasn't the norm.

An independent arm enabled advisers in direct salesforces to refer clients to their IFA arm where necessary, but retaining the client and selling its restricted products to the client wherever possible. An example was Allied Dunbar Independent Insurance and Investment Services (ADIIIS). This was particularly used for pension annuities to give clients access to the best rates. Direct sales companies often could not offer annuities so their advisers would lose clients to IFAs unless they could offer this service.

Many IFAs and appointed representatives felt that, from the perspective of attracting clients, it was more attractive to be an IFA at this time.

The temporary rise of the tied agent

Soon after polarisation was introduced, many of the larger life companies, who, of course, still wanted the guaranteed business levels which direct salesforces could give them, entered exclusive relationships with building societies and estate agents, often paying big development allowances and higher commission levels to tie the knot.

In order to pay the higher commission levels, companies had to make the products more expensive for consumers, so they were often used in parts of the market where the buyer/adviser relationship was more transactional (for instance mortgages) and also in the less affluent parts of the market where direct salesforces still dominated.

When it was all over, there were many losers. The 1988 property crash caused many estate agents to go out of business with providers footing the bill.

In the case of some, including the famous Prudential, they invested millions of pounds in buying estate agents which they often closed or sold back to the original owners at a fraction of the price they paid.

It also arguably led to mis-selling problems. Direct salespeople/advisers were given big incentives and big targets. Endowment mis-selling was the first of many scandals, although it must be said both IFAs and direct sales companies were caught up in this.

The demise of the tied agent

In the end, during the polarisation era, tied agency became the domain of the few. Tied agencies suited people involved in selling simpler products to captive audiences, so they tended to be within estate agents (many tied to Legal & General) or specialist sectors such as NFU Mutual for farming or Teachers Assurance and Police Mutual in their respective niches.

Campaign for Independent Financial Advice (CAMIFA)

A body called CAMIFA was introduced, backed by many of the major Scottish Mutual companies including Scottish Equitable, Scottish Widows, Standard Life and Scottish Life. They promoted the value of independent advice over tied or appointed representative advice. This approach was massively successful, pointing out that the best advice was to have a choice of company.

Those companies which worked with IFAs, direct sales and tied agents were excluded from CAMIFA, which had the tendency to put them on the back foot with IFAs. Eagle Star, my company, was one of these. We had a few tied agents and I remember finding many IFAs refused to support non-CAMIFA companies such as ours for a time. This was quite damaging to us.

Duncan Singer, who was a Broker Consultant with Scottish Equitable at the time, was on the other side of this experience. As he discovered, most brokers wanted to support CAMIFA companies wherever possible.

"Although part of my motivation for moving from Legal & General to Scottish Equitable was to develop my knowledge and experience of the Corporate Pensions, my main reason was the Financial Services Act, the 1986 Act.

"Many were predicting that the polarisation of the market would lead to the demise of the IFA, whereas in fact it had the opposite effect. I didn't want to become part of some kind of tied agent regime. I liked the whole concept of independent advice, and the momentum was building in favour of independence and support for life companies backing CAMIFA (who were predominately small mutuals) at the expense of the large proprietary companies most of whom ran large direct salesforces. CAMIFA had a little blue logo, and IFAs supporting CAMIFA all had these blue badges in their window to show that they were independent. I wanted to stay part of that colour."

The rise and rise of the IFA

The rise of the IFAs from the late 1980s lasted around 30 years, with two exceptions, which will be mentioned later. Here are two examples.

Lucian Russ started off as a financial planner in 1996 in City Financial Partners, a London based firm operating on an industrial scale. They were basically an old-style insurance agency firm. This is what he told me about working in Central London.

"Essentially my first job in the industry, cold calling, namely a professional model. Everybody's immaculately dressed, everybody's dreaming of having a good life, doing well and working with great

*people and wanting to get on. There were 1200 people on a sales floor.
I think we had five or six floors in CenterPoint."*

It was very much a sales environment. The role was commission only and
involved a lot of cold calling with layers of management taking a cut of the
massive commissions on offer. He said:

> *"It was actually a pyramid scheme with sales managers, area
> managers, branch managers and national managers and that sort of
> structure. We were on an incentive scheme, where you got points for
> sales. Every month we had a reward ceremony and this impacted on
> promotions. Once you got to partner level, you had a little brooch with
> little rubies on. It was a pretty classic sales organisation."*

After 18 months, he had passed a few exams including G60 (pensions). He
joined an IFA in Baker Street where he bizarrely spent four days a week
selling pensions and one day a week calculating remediation for people
who had been mis-sold pensions. This was around the year 2000/01 and
he told me:

> *"I had done all the exams and the higher exams at that point and we
> started the pension or remediation scheme so I was in charge of that
> as well as being a sales consultant. It was compensating people for
> taking them out of final sale pension schemes. My role was to go back
> and get cash equivalent pension transfer values and work out where
> they got to, and make an offer to put it right.*

> *"So, on the one hand I was advising on new business. On the other
> hand, once a week I was spending time calculating remediation and
> trying to get people back into their old schemes".*

Some of his more experienced colleagues sold big group schemes where
they would secure an agreement with an employer to put a pension scheme
in place. Lucian would go in and sign up the individuals to the scheme.

> *"You sign everybody up for the scheme and transfer them out of their
> old scheme."*

There wasn't much evidence of due diligence, nobody asked any questions, and it was very lucrative. If you're rewriting a scheme, you might be getting £50 – £200K income.

There was no real articulation of value. The usual sale was:

> "Your scheme's crap. This is what we can do. It's going to be better for investment performance, it's going to be better for charges, insurance coverage is better, it's cheaper. They all come in, we'll do all this, we'll do all that. It's not an unreasonable value proposition but it's not really articulated great, not too sophisticated."

I asked Lucian whether they acted in the client's interest? He replied, "I think there's a dual interest".

Lucian was in a city-based pension firm selling massive pension schemes for hundreds of thousands of pounds worth of commission, whereas Terry Ellis had moved on by this stage and eventually Abbey Life closed down. Compliance and Polarisation had given IFAs a significant edge. He told me what it was like when he returned to the industry in 2003. He was in a regional firm giving a price to individuals.

> "I worked for an IFA company in Leicester and things were VERY different, because then you had to do a proper full fact find and you had to show research that you were looking at what was the best policy for the client. You also had to look at what was the best company to be using for the client.

> "You also had to do a letter of suitability showing that the plan you were advising/recommending was suitable for the client. And then, when you went to present it to them, you had to declare your commission, and you had to declare all your reasons why you were recommending it, that particular product. It also had to be affordable for them; they had to sign it, to that effect."

But the more complex requirements meant IFAs had a better class of client than a typical direct sales client. Terry said:

"At Abbey Life, most associates used to do business in people's houses, selling Life Assurance, Critical Illness cover, pensions, mortgages, we used to do mortgages then a lot. All from their houses, as opposed to businesses. That worked well, because nobody else was doing it. You couldn't do business online, then you couldn't go to the bank and take out an Abbey Life policy. Abbey Life and companies like that had a monopoly over that type of policy, and there was a big need for pensions and retirement planning, as anyone who wasn't in a company scheme needed to have a pension.

"Once I became an IFA, the whole thing became a lot more up-market and we developed relationships with solicitors. So, people were doing solicitor work to do with inheritance tax and people's estates. They could take out policies in trust to cover the tax liability, so that was quite good because we would use those as a two-way relationship.

"When I became an IFA, it was more professional, and I spoke to wealthier people. I used to go and sell some investments and it used to shock me how much money people had to invest."

So IFAs began to focus on the wealthy, leaving direct salesforces and banks to focus on the less affluent clients. Of course, by focusing on the wealthier, more profitable clients, it gave greater opportunity to provide a higher quality, more client-focused service.

CHAPTER 3 SUMMARY

- Building societies and banks were some of the first introducers to life companies.

- Broker consultants were employed to convert these leads.

- Legislation drove development of the market.

- Life Assurance Premium Relief (LAPR) initially encouraged the creation of life assurance linked savings plans.

- Mortgage Interest Relief at Source (MIRAS) encouraged the sale of endowment policies.

- When LAPR & MIRAS were ended, the market survived.

- The Financial Services Act 1986 was the introduction of light-touch regulation.

- Polarisation rules favoured IFAs over direct salesforces.

- Some IFAs used direct sales tactics to grow.

- Many large life assurance companies set up 'tied agency' appointed representative networks who they funded with development allowances. They lost a lot of money when tied estate agents failed after the post-MIRAS property crash.

- Campaign for Independent Financial Advice (CAMIFA), encouraged IFAs to support product providers without their own direct salesforces or tied agents. It was an effective campaigning body and partly contributed to the success of many of the small mutual offices.

CHAPTER 4

The rise and fall of Bancassurance

I started my career in 1981 at NatWest Insurance services, a bank-owned insurance broker who provided insurance and life assurance to its customers via its banking branches. By the 1990s, several years after I had left, the banks were increasingly focused on earning commission from insurance, and naturally the next logical step was to own their own insurance companies.

Banks saw an opportunity to increase their share of 'customer wallet', and with their resources and customer base they quickly dominated until legislation priced them out of the market.

Despite the demise of the tied agent and direct sales company, St James's Place survived and so did one other specialist group of insurers: bancassurers.

Product providers were always keen to sell more and find areas of competitive advantage and in the 1990s, Bancassurance became the latest battleground.

Bancassurance, according to Investopedia is an arrangement in which insurance companies leverage on the customer base of banks to sell insurance products to banks' customers. Bancassurance is insurance provided by a bank. For example, a bank could offer life insurance in addition to its savings, loans, and investment services.

Bancassurance is spelled with a 'c' instead of a 'k' because it's an idea we imported from France where it first appeared in 1980. It was already established in Europe well before it reached the UK but could be regarded as a logical extension of its services.

By contrast, Bancassurance was illegal in the USA until 1999 because The Glass-Steagall Act of 1933 prevented the banks of the USA from entering into alliance with different financial services providers.

History

In the late 1970s and early 1980s, banks realised they could earn commission from selling products on behalf of insurance companies.

There was no doubt that banks were in a good position to sell financial products to customers. For a start, loan protection and mortgage protection are naturally easy to sell alongside loans and mortgages and it led to implied conditional selling where the bank adviser might imply the customer had to buy the bank product if they wanted the loan or mortgage.

This was an extension of the relationship I described earlier between the building societies (now mainly owned by banks) and the insurance companies in the mid-1980s.

Also, the banks had access to money markets so were no longer so dependent on deposits to fund their lending. As a result, they were happy to persuade customers to buy insurance investment bonds whereby they could earn immediate commission of 5–7% of the amount invested. They had access to customer accounts so could see when customers made large deposits from maturing policies, legacies etc, and counter staff were trained to suggest a customer making a large deposit should meet the bank's internal financial adviser.

In the UK, deregulation of banking meant new entrants and new threats for the cosy world of banks and building societies so not surprisingly they were open to new forms of income. They became insurance agents or insurance brokers. It was quite common for insurance agents to have building society agencies, so the first steps were quite limited but by the early 1980s, the banks had large, centralised insurance broking businesses which sold insurance and some financial services products through the bank branches.

Although TSB and Lloyds Bank had wholly owned insurance subsidiaries (TSB Life and Black Horse Life), it was only when NatWest Life was created in 1994 (a joint venture with Norwich Union) that Bancassurance became an important player in UK financial advice.

As a big four bank, NatWest moved from being an intermediary to being a product provider with all the cultural sales issues this created. The biggest was the culture clash between risk adverse bankers and commission hungry advisers.

My late father worked in a bank. He worked hard and progressed to the level of bank manager which was originally a well-respected and trusted position. His job was to lend money to businesses, maintain a relationship with them and to protect the bank from loans defaulting. He was, of course, cautious and we might today describe him as risk-averse.

In the later years of his career, the banks became obsessed with generating more and more income with targets for credit cards and insurance.

He told me that his bank became obsessed with selling added services – almost whether customers needed them or not. He told me targets kept rising and the pressure was growing. I saw my dad, who always loved his job, start to fall out of love with it and in 1993 he was offered, and took, early retirement. It was no longer a job requiring relationships, judgement and caution. It was a pure sales job where lending decisions were taken centrally, and the banks seemed impersonal and disinterested in their clients. Of course, as we now know, the banks were no longer cautious!

By the early 2000s, the banks were becoming obsessed with 'share of customer wallet' and Bancassurance helped them take a bigger share. This later led to the PPI mis-selling scandal which was a catastrophic failure that resulted in fines, compensation and massive reputational damage. Banks had large teams of financial advisers and the ability to introduce the financial adviser at the perfect time for a customer to buy as they had so much data on their customers and unique oversight of bank account movements and deposits.

Back in 2005 Louise Hunt was a protection manager at one of the large high street banks. Her role was working alongside the mortgage managers to increase the amount of protection sold, because most people would go to a bank for a mortgage because they have a need; they need a mortgage.

> Louise told me, "It's the difference between a want and a need. Most people don't want to pay for an insurance policy, but they do understand that there's a need to pay for that. So, it was about making sure that we were cross-selling, ultimately, but also for the client's best interest."

Louise confirmed the bank became very effective at cross-selling.

> "The banks first got their taste for wealth management. And then they did very small ISAs. It used to be quite selective, kind of cheap, low-value investments we would do in terms of £10,000–£20,000 into an ISA for a client, depending on what the ISA limits were at that point. That was the first introduction, for clients, into financial planning. Then I think, post RDR, that's when wealth planning came into its own. And there's a difference between wealth planning and investment advice. It was very easy to just put someone's money into an ISA rather than actually planning and mapping out their future and actually fundamentally changing a client's life."

I asked Louise about the type of clients she had back then and who she gave advice to.

> "It would be anyone. It would be your average Joe in the street who had worked and saved their entire life. They might have £50,000 in the bank and that is all that they've got. So, we needed to be really cautious and make sure that they were getting the best advice because

they had very little capacity for loss, in comparison to maybe some of the wealthier people out there in the market."

Bank sales income requirements were cascaded down to the bank staff in terms of target pressures. This was particularly helpful for the banks as it allowed them to survive even as commission disclosure was starting to cause problems for other financial advisers.

In a bizarre twist, Halifax Bank of Scotland (HBOS) was run by someone with a background in retail, which, it might be argued, led to an unhealthy interest in deals and a loss of focus on risk, which led to the bank's eventual collapse and takeover by Lloyds Bank – causing that bank also to collapse and be bailed out by the UK Government.

From the mid-1990s through the banking crisis in 2008, Bancassurance was a major player in financial advice and even after the banking crisis of 2008, it still continued until 2013 when it was largely wiped out by RDR.

CHAPTER 4 SUMMARY

- Banks started developing their own insurance brokers in the 1980s.

- Deregulation of UK banking created a threat to clearing banks and building societies and led them to seek new forms of income.

- The 1990s saw creation and growth of bancassurance -a concept born in Europe.

- Bancassurance was one of the big opportunities In Europe to increase their 'share of customer wallet'.

- By contrast, bancassurance was illegal in America.

- Banking moved from a job requiring relationships, judgement and caution to pure sales.

- Many bank advisers mis-sold PPI and the banks were required to pay compensation.

- It was an important part of the market from the mid-1990s to the credit crunch of 2008.

- Bancassurance was largely wiped out by RDR in 2013.

CHAPTER 5

The lead-up to RDR

The Retail Distribution review did more to professionalise the financial advice market than anything that went before it, but it also led it to the brink of a new business collapse.

The numbers of UK financial advisers authorised to give investment advice had been dropping ever since regulation was introduced in 1987. However, RDR wiped a further 20% off these numbers, and caused a 44% drop in bank-based advisers almost overnight!

While the outcome might now be regarded as positive for the profession, that wasn't necessarily apparent in the few years following.

The introduction of depolarisation in 2004 probably saved the direct salesforces because they could suddenly compete on a more even footing with the IFAs.

Depolarisation reversed the concept of polarisation which was introduced in The Financial Services Act 1987 and had disadvantaged direct salesforces so much. Whereas polarisation meant an advice business was either an IFA business with a full choice of companies or a tied agent with a sole provider and no choice, depolarisation ended this.

It allowed tied agents to 'gap-fill' with other companies' products, so it created a whole new playing field for 'restricted' companies.

While IFAs still have the benefit of being able to give best advice from across the whole market, and were often renamed 'whole-of-market IFAs', the Financial Advice and Markets Act meant that the same company could offer different offerings (whole-of-market and restricted) to the same client at different times. In some cases, groups had both an IFA and a restricted arm.

When RDR followed we really saw the results of this change.

Compliance gets teeth!

Even before RDR, Compliance became stricter as the legislation began to bite.

Many traditional 'salespeople' didn't like this. Terry told me that the job had become less salesy and more process driven.

> "Compliance – we used to call them 'the anti-sales', because it was really as if they didn't want you to make a sale! Every time I sent in a suitability letter stating what I was selling and why, there was always something wrong with it, it always kept coming back, because the compliance department were a bit anal. Everything had to be absolutely 100% right, and any one little thing that was wrong, it came back. You could spend 5 minutes selling something, and then you could spend 3 hours doing all the paperwork, all the compliance, all the research."

Even though most people recognised there was a need to protect clients, many felt the approach was over the top with reports being returned for minor as well as major reasons. And of course, many of the advisers were more sales skilled than administrative so they found it particularly hard.

Many advisers complained to me about the paperwork. Recommendation reports would be submitted for approval, examined by Compliance and returned unapproved, not only for poor advice reasons but also minor issues such as spelling and grammatical mistakes.

Like many other financial advisers brought up in the direct sales companies, this did not suit Terry. He said:

"Things were very, very, different. And it didn't particularly suit me and a lot of others like me, because I was a salesman. It was just a lot of admin."

Over time, those attracted to working in the profession changed. A lot of people came from banking backgrounds and accountancy backgrounds because *"compliance was more interested in paperwork and the admin than they were the sales sides of it."*

Eventually it drove Terry and many like him to leave the profession.

The power of distributors

Before RDR, the value of an ongoing relationship with a client was much lower than it is today. While most financial advisers were only remunerated on new business, there was very little financial incentive to stay in touch with clients once the transaction had been completed. Financial advice was usually based on a sale of a product, so key events such as the birth of a child, marriage, house purchase and inheritance would often trigger a need for protection or investments. As such, there was a growth of specialists in these particular life events (such as mortgage brokers, school fee planners and tax advisers) and often they would never return to the client.

This was particularly true of mortgage advisers who could advise on endowment mortgages, earning a considerable amount of initial commission and then move on to the next client. This was new-business-driven and although some mortgage advisors would hope clients would come back to them, on the whole there were many introducers looking to pass clients seeking a mortgage in the direction of a financial adviser in exchange for an introduction fee. The adviser would sell them an endowment and split the commission with the introducer (often resulting in the previous policy being cancelled).

Once endowments were discredited, this continued in the shape of people selling protection, which paid a very high rate of commission in comparison to the premiums paid. At a later date, mortgage providers started to encourage remortgage clients through offering procurement fees, which further enhanced the earnings for a mortgage adviser.

Despite all the above, there were some advisers who did maintain an ongoing relationship with clients and their families. In some cases, these would be insurance brokers who would maintain a relationship on the general insurance side, thus being available when the events I mentioned occurred. In many of the larger insurance brokers, they would have life and pensions sales specialists who would deal with the clients of the business as and when life and investments advice were required.

Likewise, as we have seen, the building societies and banks developed their bancassurance model. As banks and building societies are often involved at the time of life events, as previously described (new home, birth of a child, etc), they were in a very good position to pass the lead on to an in-house financial adviser who could arrange a policy on behalf of the client.

Commission disclosure

I mentioned previously that financial advisers didn't tell clients how much commission they earned on a sale. Commission Disclosure was resisted by the industry. Familiar arguments included "The shopkeeper doesn't disclose his mark-up when he sells me a Mars bar – why should I disclose the commission I earn on a policy?"

In the end it was introduced gradually. First came soft disclosure. This was when the value of commission was disclosed as a % of premiums or of the investment made. It was stated in the small print.

Then we moved to hard disclosure expressed in pounds and pence. But eventually we reached explicit disclosure when the financial adviser was compelled to openly tell their client what he or she earned in pounds and pence from the sale of a policy. It wasn't popular with advisers, but policy costs were also being driven down with the use of technology, and eventually we reached the 'One per cent World' where policy costs fell below 1% pa and advisers fully disclosed the 'commission' they earned to their clients.

Of course, this meant it was incredibly difficult to justify high initial commissions for savings plans, and client resistance naturally drove sales behaviours.

> "People like me found that quite difficult, I found it quite alien to say, "I'm starting to charge a fee", and most middle of the road customers, didn't like that. It's like going to see a solicitor or accountant and finding out how much they charge an hour."

The next logical step was the end of commission altogether.

The interim step to fees

As commission started to be regulated more heavily, some IFAs started to give clients the choice of commission or fees, and many more financial advisers started to demand ongoing trail commission for servicing a policy from the product providers so that they should move to fees gradually.

Trail commission was paid by product providers to IFAs for ongoing servicing. They typically paid a small amount – initially 0.25% or 0.5% of the policy's value every year while a policy was in force. It was designed to stop the "churning" of policies for new initial commission and for recognising the ongoing work an IFA would have to do for a client.

Many IFAs now chose to take reduced initial commission with increased trail commission. The great thing for the IFA was that it looked better when disclosing earnings to a client and not only ensured they had an ongoing income, but also, they could maintain an ongoing relationship with the clients.

This trail commission was non-contractual, which did give the industry problems down the line. In some cases, we saw IFAs persuading clients to sign their trail commission over to them and away from the previous adviser.

This created a lot of upset. If an adviser chose to take trail commission but no or low initial commission, they saw trail commission as part of the remuneration for arranging the advice in the first place, but its legal position was that trail fees were for the ongoing relationship only. This meant that a new adviser could step in, persuade the client to sign the trail commission over to them and the initial adviser could lose out.

There are two sides to this argument. On the one side, the new adviser could legitimately claim that the client was happy to sign across their trail commission because they weren't happy with the ongoing service provided by the original advisor. But, on the other side, the original adviser might well argue that most of the work has to be done at the time initial advice was given and that trail commission was just a way of allowing the client to spread the cost.

It wasn't an ideal situation, but for those watching carefully, it probably set the scene for the early post-RDR period when some advisers seemed to effortlessly collect client assets under management with their ongoing trail fees while the ceding advisers appeared to be looking the other way.

CHAPTER 5 SUMMARY

- Regulation had first been introduced in the 1987 Financial Services Act.

- Polarisation was introduced at the same time and helped the growth of IFAs.

- Depolarization was introduced in 2004, which probably saved the direct salesforces, allowing them to gap-fill and more closely compete with IFAs.

- Compliance became stricter over time.

- Traditional sales-led financial advisers struggled with compliance. Many sales-led advisers left the profession.

- Dependence on commission gave distributors power to influence advisers. New business commission also drove bad behaviours.

- Commission disclosure came in stages and policy costs started to drop.

- Trail commission was an initial step into fees but that also created a lot of upset as it encouraged poaching of clients.

CHAPTER 6

The arrival and impact of RDR

The main impact of the Retail Distribution Review was to raise the barrier to entry for financial advisers through the need for higher qualifications, but simultaneously ended commissions on investment products, thus reducing the financial adviser's ability to earn.

Let's look at both of these areas, starting with qualifications.

When RDR was implemented, the minimum qualification for a financial adviser rose from QCF level 3 (FPC) to QCF level 4 (originally called the Advanced Financial Planning Certificate (AFPC) but now called the Diploma). An existing financial adviser giving investment advice had to pass the qualification and apply for and receive a Statement of Professional Standing (SPS) before 1st January 2013 if they were to continue.

In the past, it has taken regulation to persuade many financial advisers to pass their exams. Although I completed the AFPC – now the Dip PFS – in 1992, even 20 years later, in the lead-up to RDR, when the bar was raised, those with full diploma were in the minority, so it took a monumental effort to get the industry up to this minimum standard.

The Qualifications and Curriculum Authority (QCA) says a level 4 qualification is equivalent to year 1 of a bachelor's degree. The most common qualifications would typically be:

- Diploma in Financial Planning (Dip CII or Dip PFS) from the CII/PFS;
- Diploma for Financial Advisers (Dip FA) from the London Institute of Banking and Finance;
- For non-regulated people such as mortgage advisers, the most common qualification is CeMap. This is a level 3 qualification.

In 2012, in the lead-up to RDR, a high percentage of financial advisers had not yet passed it or any of its equivalents. Many adviser businesses and companies had to ensure all their advisers reached level 4 if they wanted to continue. It was not easy, and many product providers offered free training. Of course, many were not able or chose not to take the exams.

Despite the challenges we saw of getting the financial planning profession up to level 4 qualifications, increasingly today, the new generation of planners are choosing to move beyond the minimum.

Many financial advisers are adding to their qualifications by taking extra exams to reach level 6. The most common being chartered financial planners (APFS, ACII., Adv DipFA), chartered fellows (FPFS) chartered wealth managers (ACISI) (for those managing investments) and level 7 certified financial planners (CFP). Nowadays, many financial advice companies encourage staff to reach these higher qualification levels. We are also seeing an increase in specialist qualifications such as SOLLA (Society of Later Life Advisers).

The end of commission on investment products

Investment products could be pensions or it could be investments. Financial advice in this context means investment advice.

Mortgages and protection were now separated out and referred to as non-regulated as they were under less strenuous regulations and commission payments continued.

Typical commission structures for an IFA (pre RDR)

- A previous criticism of the old systems was that an IFA might receive a higher level of commission from one company than another. So, in the commission regime, advisers made most of their money from the sale of savings and pension plans plus investment bonds.
- Despite claims of the opposite, insurance companies raised commission rates several times in the 1990s and 2000s in an attempt to increase sales. Starting initially with Life Assurance and Unit Trust Regulatory Organisation (LAUTRO) rates, uplifts were added by most companies from time to time and commission payment levels were a key part of every broker consultant's armoury (often in exchange for a minimum level of support).

Example of savings commission pre RDR

A famous example of that would be a Scottish Widow's Endowment plan 10. This was a 20-year contract dressed up as a 10-year contract, thus having the benefit of paying 20-year commission (which was twice the amount payable on a 10-year plan) to an adviser. Needless to say, the Scottish Widows Endowment plan 10 sold very well through financial advisers before RDR while other companies' 10-year savings plans were left on the shelf!

Typical post-RDR fee structure for IFAs using an Assets Under Advice basis (AUA)

Fees are typically:

- Initial – up to 3% of the initial investment;
- Ongoing – 0.5% to 1%;
- For savings plans the fees are similar;
- Commission v Fees.

Product	Typical Commission (Pre 2013)	Typical Fees (post 2013) for businesses using an AUA model
Unit Trusts	3% initial only	Up to 3% initial + 0.5% – 1.0% ongoing
Investment bonds	5.25%– 5.75% initial + 0.25% trail	Up to 3% initial + 0.5% – 1.0% ongoing
Offshore bonds	Up to 7% initial	Up to 3% initial + 0.5% – 1.0% ongoing
Savings plans	Up to 55% initial	0.5% – 1.0% ongoing
Low-cost Endowment Policies	Up to 69% initial + 2.5% trail	Not applicable
Pension plans	25% – 55% initial + 2.5% trail	0.5 to 1.0% ongoing. 1% – 3% on lump sums
Pension transfers	4%	3% – 4% or fixed fee

When RDR was introduced, the effect on an IFA firm was massive. As can be seen from the table above. A £100 per month savings plan would now pay £36 – 48 in the first year compared to previously paying up to £828 in the first year. It would take an IFA a long time to build this into a meaningful income, so for someone who also needed to gain advanced qualifications, selling savings plans became less attractive.

Not surprisingly, the aim is now to advise people with large lump sums to invest and the emphasis has moved to ongoing income through client servicing. So, the target has changed from a young saver to an older person or couple with significant assets built up already.

Let me go back to Terry again:

> "Everything had changed. The fees on regular premium pensions went right down, and people stopped selling pensions because the fees were so low, which is ridiculous, but that's exactly what happened. In the old days a lot of saving schemes, life assurance and pensions were front-end loaded and it made it worthwhile for the salesperson. The financial services authority thought that was wrong, so they changed it all – commission on regular premium plans is a lot less so the emphasis went onto lump sums."

So, with regular premium policies now paying very little to the advisers, many financial advisers realised they could no longer earn a living from 'ordinary' clients.

Impact of RDR on the financial planning profession

The end of commission totally broke the relationship between product providers and financial advisors with very few exceptions.

It meant for the majority of financial advisers that there was no product bias. In the case of an IFA, they will charge a fee to the client and this will not vary according to the company whose products they recommend.

Sunset clause

Despite the end of commission on new products advised on, initially, financial advisers were allowed to continue collecting trail commission on products sold in the past, but eventually this too was ended.

What really happened during RDR?

RDR was the biggest change in a generation.

Despite the fact that the level 4 diploma had been introduced in the early 1990s (then called the Advanced Financial Planning Certificate), a high proportion of financial advisers still harked back to the sales driven era and had not embraced the higher qualification level so many companies felt they had to focus on helping financial advisers gain the new qualification minimum. I don't know whether they thought the end of commission was less important, but many seemed to ignore this challenge – almost hoping it would go away.

Many financial advisers either chose, or were forced, to leave the profession. Many more chose to stay on as mortgage and protection advisers, which was known as non-regulated (although less regulated would have been a better description).

With the end of commission on investment products, many interpreted the legislation to imply that a client would be required to pay two cheques to an adviser – one for the investment and a second one for the advice. No-one knew how many clients would be willing to pay this way.

Most companies feared a collapse in sales from which they would struggle to recover. Many were right to fear it.

I recall a situation which surprised and worried me. In the lead-up to RDR, one of our client companies operating in the restricted world was keen to understand what incentive schemes their competitors were planning after RDR.

As an Executive Search Firm, we are often commissioned by companies to conduct market research for them. This is usually market benchmarking for salaries, bonus schemes or sales targets. However, this proved to be probably the toughest research assignment we ever took on.

As we researched the market, it became apparent to us that hardly any company had come up with an adequate way to remunerate its advisers after RDR because the regulations seemed designed to end any form of sales incentive.

Most advice businesses recognised they needed a minimum fee per year from each customer (usually £1,000 - £2,000). Quite quickly it became apparent that customers making small transactional purchases - small investments and pensions - were unwilling to pay this amount.

This hastened the demise of Bancassurance, whose customers were unwilling to pay for financial advice when buying products which had previously seemed free. It also encouraged the banks to focus on selling non-regulated products such as mortgages and protection policies where commission was still allowed rather than charge all but their most wealthy clients for investment advice.

One particular extreme example I recall, was AXA Bancassurance which closed quite quickly after RDR, resulting in 450 redundancies.

In the early 2000s, AXA, like many product providers, saw the threat to the company if independent financial advisers chose to no longer sell their products; so they had built a number of banking ties, and supplied an outsourced Bancassurance adviser force to quite a few of the smaller banks.

The common industry term for this was 'rent a rep'. AXA's Bancassurance team was focused on selling wealth products and when RDR was introduced, the new rules didn't work for them. They tried various remuneration schemes, such as targeting and remunerating their bancassurance advisers for the number of plans sold, but that just led to financial advisers selling a high number of low value plans.

Soon after RDR was implemented, AXA closed its Bancassurance division and the other banks followed course.

For those people who did remain in Bancassurance, the experience was also very sobering as Louise Hunt, who was at a leading clearing bank, explained to me.

Louise remembers it well.

> "There was a big round of redundancies. For those who stayed, there was a lot of uncertainty. There was a lot of the old school financial planners that had an easy ride of it for a long time, not liking the move away from a bonus scheme that was driven through sales. Now there was more of an annualised, profit-based bonus scheme.

> "Salaries increased and bonuses went down. So that way people had a good cost-of-living base from their salary. You were no longer able to generate the huge bonuses which were possible before RDR. And I think that's the biggest change that happened for the advisers, and not all of it went down that well. We gradually moved from monthly and quarterly bonuses to six-monthly bonuses to annual bonuses. That was a big change for a lot of the FPs. But I do think that it was the right thing to do."

Louise said it was not a happy time for successful Bancassurance advisers, but those who had the opportunity to remain in position did so. She told me:

> "Despite everything, very few chose to leave. Mainly because of the whole market crashing and businesses closing."

She reminded me that the other clearing banks also closed their financial advice arms, so people were thankful and grateful to still have a job.

So, there we have it. Banks dominated the financial advice sector for around 20 years; then, once the customer had to choose to pay openly for financial advice, they were gone!

Since that time the banks have concentrated on transactional non-regulated business such as mortgage and loan protection and also most have a high and ultra-high net worth financial advice and fund management offering aimed at their wealthier clients.

Finally, the banks have come full circle, with a creation of a joint venture between Schroders and Lloyds bank. More on that later.

The end of the road?

The end of commission was a costly business for an IFA previously dependent on indemnity commission. This was particularly relevant to those who sold a lot of new business based on saving (regular premium pension plans etc). Although a move to a fee model might be more rewarding in the long term, but only if they could afford a near 100% loss of new business income on day one.

I mentioned in a previous chapter that in the lead-up to RDR many financial advice businesses had tried to wean themselves off of indemnity commission, but the impact was still massive when it came.

Over the previous 30 years, we had seen a 90% decline in financial adviser numbers. In 1986, just before the financial services act was implemented, there were reputed to be 300,000 UK financial advisers (Source FT Adviser 11/2/2016).

According to money marketing, in 2011 there were 40,511 financial advisers which dropped 24% to 31,132 in the 2-year lead-up to RDR. When RDR was introduced, the number of financial advisers dropped even faster.

In the first 3 months after RDR, the official FSA figures[1] showed a 20% drop in financial advisers and a 44% drop in bank advisers.

---

1   *Source Money Marketing 27/3/2013 "First official RDR stats: adviser numbers down 20% bank advisers fall 44%"

And the shocking truth was that, for a while after RDR lesser qualified mortgage brokers often earned much more than their higher qualified financial adviser equivalents.

Shortly after RDR, I recall attending a mortgage exhibition with a client. We had been retained to find a Mortgage Director to build a mortgage division for them. I attended the event to network and identify possible 'movers and shakers' in the market who might be ready for a new challenge and be attracted to our exciting new role. Our client was offering equity participation as well as a six-figure basic salary, so I anticipated having a good choice of candidates. I was really shocked to quickly realise that we had underestimated the salary we would need to offer.

The individuals I spoke to were earning much more than their better qualified colleagues who had remained in the financial advice market. Whereas wealth salaries had dropped significantly following RDR, the opposite had happened in the mortgage market where large players had turned their focus and procurement fees had risen to create a fees battle between lenders – and salaries for those in the sector were sky-rocketing. Suffice to say, our client reset the package and we were eventually successful in securing their dream candidate, albeit at a much higher than anticipated salary!

Many financial adviser companies closed or hunkered down – or focused on protection sales as they waited for the storm to pass.

Reflections on RDR and the end of the commission era

Even though it was only a few years ago, the pre-RDR era seems a million miles away from where we are now.

Although we all believed in helping customers achieve better financial outcomes, the profession grew based on acquiring salespeople whose behaviours were driven by commissions for securing new business. The system of hiring people on a self-employed basis also encouraged advisers to make the most profitable decision for them.

Financial advice is not easy for a lay person to challenge and many sales practices such as churning policies (selling new ones and cancelling old ones) or choosing to sell the product which paid the most commission were an inevitable consequence of the system.

I asked Terry Ellis to reflect on the end of the commission era. Did he think commission drove the wrong sales behaviours?

> "Definitely yes. There were certain people who would just sell the policy that would get the most commission and whether they thought it was right or wrong, that's what used to happen really."

Terry also said that commission disclosure made things tougher.

> "Towards the end of it, I found it extremely stressful. Because I was getting a bit older you had to declare all your commission, I used to find that very difficult. We used to have to say, "for doing this pension transfer for you, my commission will be £2,000". I used to find it difficult to do that. I did actually lose a few sales as soon as I said that. When I went away it would be cancelled very quickly, and I knew that was the reason. I used to think that that part of it was very unfair, because if you're buying a car or a suit or whatever you're buying they don't have to declare how much money they're making, do they."

Quite recently, Terry saw this from the client's side in a post-RDR world when his dad received financial planning from an IFA in later life.

> "When my dad was getting advised by an IFA at the end of his life, I saw the other side of that. My dad paid a fee as opposed to a commission, and I thought it was well worth it. It was around 2% of the whole investment, which I thought was good. My dad didn't like spending any money! But I thought it was pretty good value really!"

Terry's view is that the difference between then and now is the type of client. The mass market clients he worked with can no longer afford financial advice. Those who do use financial advisers have more wealth and are happy to pay for it.

So, on the eve of RDR, in December 2012, with the financial advice industry on the verge of collapse and many financial advice businesses finding their clients unwilling to pay their fees, the financial planning profession faced its darkest hour.

CHAPTER 6 SUMMARY

- RDR increased the barrier to entry for financial advisers and reduced their ability to earn.

- The minimum qualification was raised from level 3 FPC to a level 4 Diploma in Financial Planning or equivalent.

- It ended commissions on investment products.

- The end of commission typically reduced first year's earnings on a savings plan by over 90%.

- The new remuneration system meant the focus was on wealthy clients with lump sums to invest rather than ordinary clients wanting to purchase savings and pension plans.

- Many companies set a minimum fee per year from each client.

- Once asked to pay a fee, most transactional clients chose not to do so.

- Bancassurers either cut back dramatically or left the market.

- Many financial advisers chose to become mortgage and protection advisers -where commission was still payable.

- The end of commission led to an exodus of financial advisers in the market.

- Within three months of RDR, the financial advice market was on the brink of collapse.

PART 2

The recovery

---

1 January 2013 – the day that the Retail Distribution Review was implemented, commission on investment products was outlawed, and many felt the market was on the brink of disaster.

That still wasn't the low point. In the following three months, 25% of the already depleted number of financial advisers left the market and 40% of the bank assurance advisers ceased giving investment advice or retired.

So, in part two of my book, I outline how the industry recovered from its downward spiral, leading to what I refer to as its coming of age, when it effectively became a modern profession, placing the client at the heart, aligning the adviser's interest with the client's interest.

I show how the profession was massively helped by George Osborne's decision to introduce pension freedoms and, perhaps most surprisingly how many would say the regulator 'turned a blind eye' to the market leader, allowing advisers to draw their income from clients' investments. I explain how these unexpected changes seemed to work well alongside the RDR rules, ensuring that established businesses were able to carve themselves out a profitable future.

Once the profession had come of age, of course, everything started to calm down. The businesses that had remained were largely still short of cash, but had survived.

After treading water for a number of years, the profession started to change its models.

Financial planning businesses started to look more like other professional services businesses, with increased emphasis on client reviews and servicing. That meant more back-office staff, computerisation and a structure which gave clients a much higher standard of service. Financial advisers and planners started to focus on spending more time in front of clients, often with support from paraplanners. There was a fundamental change from the old self-employed adviser model to the more modern employed advisor model, and now ownership of the client relationship rested with the firm.

As the market started, I explain how, once financial advice businesses started to become more profitable, there was a need to regrow a profession which had declined by over 90% in the last 35 years.

I have dedicated 5 chapters of the book to look at what I believe is the battleground of the future, people and processes

Three of the chapters are focused on people. Financial advice is currently a people service and I think that will remain the case. So, I focus on the talent pool, attracting the next generation of financial advisers, and finally the long-standing case for employed v self-employed financial advisers.

The talent pool looks at the ageing adviser population and the barriers to entry.

I then examine how to attract and retain the next generation of financial advisers and highlight many of the barriers we need to overcome to prevent people joining the profession.

In my final 'people' chapter, I examine both new employed and self-employed models and the parts of the industry which favour the two.

I have then dedicated a chapter to processes and working methods with the inevitable nod towards digitalisation.

In a highly regulated environment where new business creates little short-term reward in comparison with the pre-RDR period, I look at processes and working methods, including how companies are attempting to utilise modern working methods and digitalisation to keep advice costs low, while, in most cases, ensuring clients still deal with people rather than machines.

After many years in the doldrums, financial advice and wealth management businesses are now 'sexy'. It seems like everyone is after them. Their value is rising because there are more buyers than sellers. Mergers and acquisitions in financial planning are not new, but the activity has accelerated. In my mergers and acquisitions chapter I explain how this has come about and where, I believe, the market is going. We have already touched upon the fact that private equity houses have entered the sector, but I also explain why product providers are paying a premium price to acquire some financial advice firms.

In the final chapter, I outline how far we've come. In the recent past, financial adviser businesses had very little value. Today, the mergers and acquisitions market has ensured even the smallest adviser businesses can generate at least a seven-figure sum on sale and there's an active market for buying and selling businesses. This gives us optimism for the future, if we can only find a way of attracting young people to join it at a rate faster than the older advisers leave it.

Finally, like every good book, I want to leave you, the reader, with hope. You'll see that when you get there!

CHAPTER 7

The profession comes of age

St James's Place, the company many IFAs loved to hate, led the way in the recovery.

The withdrawal of commission ended the interdependent financial relationship between life companies and IFAs, but there was an anomaly in the restricted world.

At the beginning most providers seem to have assumed that product providers would no longer be able to pay advisers, and advisers would have to charge the fee directly to clients (by separate cheque) but it quickly became apparent this was not the case at St James's place.

It might be argued that St James's Place's greatest contribution to the Financial Advice industry was to persuade the regulator that its partners could deduct the fee from the product rather than having a separate payment. For many, this was commission in all but name. What it means is that when a client invests in a product or fund, the client can make a single payment to the company and the company will make initial and ongoing payments back to the partner (St James's Place title for a self-employed financial adviser). This is usually a percentage of funds invested. This may not have been what the act intended but, with the bells of doom ringing, the regulator appeared to give this approach its blessing.

Many might have expected other companies and advisers to cry foul at this point. Many didn't like the flash sales culture at the company and were ready to object... but held back from doing so.

St James's Place had become the largest player in the marketplace, and the market was collapsing around us. I think most product providers felt that if St James's Place could get away without upsetting the regulator, so could they.

Whereas previously most product providers had taken the view they didn't like the way St James's Place rewarded its advisers, at a point when the industry looked near collapse the other providers decided to copy them and effectively offered all financial advice businesses a route forward to profitability. While it involved some paperwork, it was more attractive than the alternative.

It probably helped that many companies attempting to deal with the end of commission, had seen an industry exodus as financial advisers left the profession in their droves.

So, the big product providers fell into line, allowing financial advisers to draw down ongoing fees from client funds with the regulator's blessing and the financial adviser industry was saved.

It could be argued that it still ended adviser bias as all platforms and product providers offer this system which protects the adviser from accusations of provider bias.

Of course, not all financial advisers choose to be remunerated in this way. Some do invoice fees directly from their clients, but today many adviser businesses are remunerated by deducting their initial and ongoing fees from the platforms on which their clients' money is invested.

So, for a typical small financial advice business with two financial adviser principals, one administrator and one paraplanner and £60M assets under advice, the total income might be £600,000 pa. This figure might be ongoing adviser fees (charged at 0.75%) of £450,000 and a further £150,000 initial fees.

So, once a business is established, income has a degree of certainty and tends to rise each year, making it more robust and more able to hire staff. In many cases the ongoing adviser fee income might be expected to increase each year, thus giving the two principals a valuable and increasing asset which can be sold on when they choose to retire.

How the industry adapted and recovered

After RDR in 2013, and once the new remuneration system was fully established, the profession really started changing rapidly.

Whereas before that date, the main life assurance companies had an important part to play in the market because, it could be argued, most IFAs and brokers were dependent on them for commission, once commission ended, even if they were using the Assets Under Management adviser fee model, IFAs and most multi-tied advisers had much more freedom in the type of products they could advise on.

There are now also very high barriers to entry in the profession. It is not easy to get diploma qualified and the process is quite expensive and time consuming. It is estimated to cost £6,500 to train a financial adviser just to get them authorised.

The combination of an attractive remuneration system where income generally rose every year based on rising stock markets and high barriers to entry which meant the shrinking group of authorised financial advisers had more than enough wealthy clients to go around drove up remuneration for those who remained.

Financial advisers were no longer seen as commission-generating machines but now started to be seen for what they are; valued and trusted technically competent people who have their clients' best interest at heart; and, in most cases, are not compromised by dependence on life assurance companies for their income.

This was also the era of the investment platform. Investment platforms gave asset managers and other investment managers greater access to the market, and most platforms offered a very wide variety of funds from a very wide variety of fund managers. RDR also put advisers in control.

Companies had been working on these for a long time, the earliest entrants in the UK being James Hay and Transact, plus fund supermarkets Cofunds and Fidelity FundsNetwork. When they were upgraded, the true second-generation platforms such as Cofunds and Fidelity FundsNetwork offered clients the choice of investments from a variety of asset managers and discretionary fund managers.

Much like the power of retailers in other sectors such as food supermarkets, the power seemed to be moving from the product providers to the distributors. IFA groups and financial planning groups were still the main route to market for many traditional providers, but now financial advisers could go to the full range of people in the knowledge that they should decide what was best for their clients and were not beholden to any company for its commission.

Likewise, the unbreakable link between product providers and IFAs was destroyed, with many provider companies and asset managers very concerned about how they could generate new business going forward when the advisor no longer had a dependent relationship with them.

These new financial advisers now had the freedom to work closely with their clients to decide what was best for them. Whereas, in the past, the funds market was dominated by 'with profit' bonds and a small number of company-managed funds, which might be invested in a mix of equities, property and fixed interest, this now changed. In many cases it was as easy to access a small esoteric fund as it was to access a mainstream fund, and the typical client portfolio might consist of a very high number of funds, either as part of a managed portfolio service or overseen by a discretionary fund manager.

It also led to a change in how financial advisers saw their own role in advising a client. As life and legislation became more complex, there was perhaps less need for IFAs to focus on fund management. Gradually they started to outsource this requirement through use of a centralised investment proposition, often managed by a Discretionary Fund Manager (DFM) or similar. Now the adviser became more of a financial planner, helping clients plan for the future and allowing fund choice and management to be left to the experts.

The nature of the market also changed with the end of polarisation. Being a restricted adviser now has very little impact on the choice of fund managers available. Most of the major companies offering a restricted option still had access to most of the fund managers through their platform.

Obviously, the product providers were very worried about loss of distribution and many of the larger ones started to build their own financial advice businesses. Product providers opened up new direct distribution channels, often giving an element of choice to customers while ensuring the majority of money was invested through their own platforms, products and funds.

Having seen the success of St James's Place, Old Mutual (now Quilter) started to acquire IFA networks including Positive Solutions, Intrinsic, Blueprint, Caerus and others. These networks contained many small financial planning businesses.

They also started to build private client businesses.

- Standard Life established 1825 – a private client business.
- Old Mutual (later renamed Quilter) established Quilter Private Client Advisers.
- Towry Law was acquired by Tilney bringing together a large fund management group with a large financial planning group. Later, Smith & Williamson was also merged to create Tilney, Smith & Williamson and renamed to Evelyn Partners in 2022.

At the end of 2019, one of the UK's largest global asset managers, Schroders, entered a joint venture with Lloyds Banking Group (which included Scottish Widows) to create Schroders Personal Wealth, a modern take on Bancassurance.

The impact of RDR – shock therapy for the financial advice profession

The initial effect was to rapidly reduce the number of financial advisers. However, after a big drop, numbers steadied and have now started to rise again. As of 31st December 2021, the FCA reports that there are 27,839 authorised financial advisers in the UK. However, due to the adviser demographic, the industry is struggling to appoint new financial advisers as fast as the old ones are leaving.

I explained earlier that direct sales companies such as St James's Place may have appeared to continue with a similar model and just changed the title from commission to fees. For many IFAs there was a greater divergence from this model.

The end of commission and the launch of fees meant that there was a massive change in remuneration shape. While fees can vary, and some charge on a per hour or per transaction fixed fee basis, many still relate their ongoing trail fees to assets under management, which means they can rise if the value of a customer's investments rise (and conversely fall when they fall). The upside of this is that in a rising market where an IFA or financial planner looks after their clients well, they can expect a steadily rising income. By staying in contact with the client and providing ongoing advice (the Financial Services and Market Act insists that customers have periodic reviews), the financial adviser retains a much closer ongoing relationship with the client and is aware, through the periodic review, when the client's circumstances change.

Also, in a society where wealth is cascaded through generations, there is an opportunity for a financial planner to maintain his or her relationship with a family when the money transfers to the beneficiaries.

It is this change which has presented a fantastic opportunity to the new breed of financial advisers after RDR.

The ongoing relationship with the client and the ongoing adviser fee means that clients have an ongoing value and that, of course, means that financial planning businesses have an ongoing value.

One of the first companies to recognise and realise the benefits of this were Peter Hargreaves and Stephen Lansdown of Hargreaves Lansdown, now one of the UK's largest financial services businesses. This couple of entrepreneurs created many initiatives which eventually trickled into the mainstream financial adviser community.

One example is client segmentation, allowing different clients to have different levels of service dependent on needs and budget, from full face-to-face advice right the way down to execution-only transactions.

How the life assurance companies and other product providers have adapted

Back in the early 2000s, everyone knew what a life assurance company was: it insured your life and paid out on early death. From the 1950s onwards, these companies also offered savings plans and by the 1980s, many would say they were best known as managing people's money through investment bonds and pensions. However, with RDR, we have seen the life assurance companies lose their ability to influence advisers through use of commission, and over time IFAs started to use these newfound freedoms.

Firstly, a new entrant into the market no longer had to offer a complete range of products to keep its salesforce happy. Now, even restricted advisers used more than one product.

A big battleground has been the use of technology to drive down costs.

As a general rule, most investment products use some sort of investment platform with digital access to hundreds of funds from different fund managers. Increasingly, investments and pensions would be held in a product wrapper which was authorised and met the regulatory requirements. This gave each financial adviser an almost boundaryless choice of products, platforms, funds and investment solutions. Even the restricted advisers could offer a choice of funds and products.

As such, the battleground shifted. No longer did financial advisers rely on a narrow choice of funds. Instead, they could create a centralised investment proposition (CIP) overseen by an investment committee.

The amount of dependence an adviser business places on adviser fees varies. The main source of income for a financial advice business may indeed be financial advice fees, but its parent company may well earn income from elsewhere in the value chain – for instance, shared platform fees, custody fees and investment fees.

Pension freedoms

Traditionally, money in a pension was locked away throughout a person's working life and used in retirement to purchase an annuity – an ongoing payment which would be payable until death – and sometimes beyond, in the case of a widow's/widower's pension.

If the company provided the pension, there was no need for an authorised financial adviser, as company advice does not benefit from consumer protection. If an individual purchased a pension, a financial adviser took commission on initial premiums paid and any increases, and a small commission on annuity advice provided on retirement, but when commission ended there appeared to be little incentive for financial advisers to be involved. The whole process didn't really require a financial adviser. George Osborne changed all that.

George Osborne identified a way of people accessing this asset. For quite a while it had been possible to start drawing down a personal pension fund within a self-invested pension plan, for a period before purchasing an annuity (which had to happen by age 75). This was called pension drawdown.

What many people started to think is, "my pension pot is my money. Why can't I access the whole amount if I want? Also, why should my pension fund die with me?"

By a quirk, someone dying while in drawdown before the age of 75, could already pass the balance of their fund to their beneficiaries – so a campaign to allow all people to have drawdown instead of an annuity which would die with them had already been rumbling for some time when George Osborne introduced Pension Freedoms to the Budget 2015.

The key changes were:

- Annuity purchase was no longer compulsory (even at age 75);
- The whole pension pot can be withdrawn subject to tax (over age 55);
- More flexibility on income drawdown (no maximum);
- Better death benefits. SIPP payments were free of Inheritance Tax.

For many people in company schemes, their pension fund is their second biggest asset after their house, and even the fund required to fund a modest pension can be quite substantial. At retirement, a typical couple might have funds of £500,000 + requiring advice. Increasingly, those people who are inheriting these assets are already in their 50s and already established so they're likely to retain at least part of that asset.

These people needed ongoing advice on these pension assets, and the modern fund-based advice fees made this very lucrative. Not only that, but the fees could also be charged year after year and even continue after death if the investments were cascaded through the family. Of course, any business with a predictable ongoing revenue stream has a value and that led to opportunities galore (but also headaches) for the financial planning profession.

CHAPTER 7 SUMMARY

- While others claim they contributed to the decision, St James's Place led the way.

- They secured approval from the regulator to deduct adviser fees from the investment product, rather than the client having to make a separate payment.

- With many advice businesses on the verge of collapse, the product providers followed this approach with regulators' apparent blessing.

- This created ongoing income known as ongoing advisor fees (OAF).

- OAF gave adviser businesses greater value.

- A significant portion of all advisers now use the Assets Under Advice (AUA) model.

- The power moved from providers to distributors.

- Some of the large product providers started to acquire IFA businesses to protect their position.

- Many of the largest adviser businesses became restricted, but maintained access to a wide choice of fund managers for their clients.

- After a rapid collapse in financial adviser numbers, the profession finally began to 'bottom out' around 8 years later.

- The introduction of pensions freedoms by George Osborne's budget enabled advisers, to advise their clients (and charge ongoing adviser fees) throughout retirement.

CHAPTER 8

Where we are now

Following all the changes to the financial advice industry over the last 50 years or so, we've ended up in a significantly different place to where we started. Whereas Winston Churchill was telling people that everyone should insure themselves, as the demographic has changed, asset preservation and growth has become more important.

Firstly, let's look at clients. They are wealthier than ever, and there's more demand for financial advice than ever. Baby boomers are becoming septuagenarians. As it becomes a highly regulated industry, clients are very well protected and if anything goes wrong, they can claim through the ombudsman or the FSCS.

These people have grown their wealth through the growth in house prices, pension values and technology, and many are now handing that on to the next generation. So, we're no longer just talking about protecting your family from eventualities; we're talking about protecting and building wealth that's been inherited or built due to the revaluing of assets and a healthy stock market.

Alongside this, the quality of financial advice available has risen. The high barriers to entry in terms of qualification and regulation mean only those really committed remained. A friend of mine calls it the end of dabbling. Until RDR, it was common to see financial advisers who dabbled in financial advice while having other jobs as well. They might run an estate agency or lettings agency and have an agency with Allied Dunbar on the side. They often weren't capable of or interested in getting level 4 qualified and left the profession when RDR took place.

Regulations ensured that the focus is no longer on sales of new business, but increasingly on helping clients look after and grow their wealth. It's facilitating life planning to ensure that people can plan their future around events and maybe family needs. It's helping people to understand that wealth can be cascaded down through the generations and that the middle classes may have the chance to practise what the upper classes did previously. And in this environment, demand for advice is still rising by five to seven per cent per year at a time when most advisers are reaching retirement ages.

Financial advice firms still find it difficult to retain assets through the generations. As clients die, there is research that suggests the younger generation not only like to spend the money but, also, don't necessarily follow their parents and grandparents by using the same adviser. This will change, as financial advice businesses learn better how to maintain relationships and manage generational transfer of assets from their clients to their families.

One way to achieve this is to offer a wider range of services, which help the younger generation. For example, while the older generation may mainly need inheritance tax advice and wealth management, some of the younger generation may be seeking mortgage advice, will writing, and family protection.

As firms become larger, they are more able to offer this range of services, which gives them a stronger client proposition and more chance of maintaining the relationship through the generations.

We're already starting to see that many financial planners recognise that looking after your money is not the only thing they should be doing for you. People have aspirations and, really, money is only a way of achieving the lifestyle they want. A good life planner/financial planner is in a much better position to help you plan out your future than just a 'traditional style' financial adviser. I recently recommended my financial planner to a friend, and it became apparent that he is advising all three generations with the things that matter most to them in life. He is positioning his business well and should benefit from the foresight he has shown.

New ways of working

Secondly, let's look at the industry itself.

The IFA market is extremely fragmented, and many would call it a cottage industry. 90% of financial planning businesses have fewer than five financial planners. Only one per cent has 50 or more financial planners. Compared to other professions, such as solicitors and accountants, this is a very skewed model.

Despite the above, 50% of all financial planners work for the top one per cent in terms of team size.

Even though, over the past few years, the use of financial planning firms has risen as people recognise that ongoing value. Most clients pay ongoing fees, which can be reasonably predicted, and, in many cases, will rise as the value of assets in the management rise.

There are still some major issues.

Financial advisers' reputation

There has always been a question over the reputation of financial advisers. Going right back to the 1950s and '60s, when the 'man from the Pru' was extremely trusted, but some of the lesser companies weren't. From the dawn of the unit-linked life assurance direct sales era through the 1960s, '70s, '80s, and '90s where the flash life insurance salesman with the shiny shoes and nice car appeared to have more interest in incentive trips and commissions than they did in their clients. Through to the 2000s and beyond as regulation bit, and post 2013 when RDR undoubtedly raised the standards, quality, and qualifications of advisers alongside implementing massive consumer protection.

Despite that, the financial adviser profession can still have a seedy reputation. Back in the 1980s and '90s, there was undoubtedly a drinking culture when the life inspectors (broker consultants) entertained financial advisers. I remember an era when some of our top broker consultants spent all afternoon, several times a week in the pub with their IFAs.

I also remember various pyramid schemes sold by companies such as Porchester Life, General Portfolio and others, to encourage advisers to join them with promises of shares in the company in exchange for commission. Of course, these shares often amounted to nothing.

Why does this matter?

Because if you look at the way that the youth of today regard financial advice, they do so with suspicion. Despite loads of efforts to the contrary, market feedback and studies by the FCA show that most young people do not want to work in financial advice.

The structure of a modern financial planning business

I recently interviewed a senior manager in a major financial advice business who summed up how structures of businesses have changed in the past 30 years.

Back in the 1990s, he and two of his friends left Pearl Assurance together and set up an independent financial adviser business. There was no division of labour and all three were salespeople/financial advisers so all three just carried on working as they had before. However, even by the 1990s, this model was starting to change.

They quickly realised that they could not grow their business without agreeing management responsibilities. Arguments followed about administration and compliance. He said openly to me that having three advisers together just did not work and eventually the three friends parted.

Today a small financial advice business will certainly have a division between financial advice and operations. As the business grows, the role of Compliance (or Chief Risk) Officer will also be separated out.

For a slightly larger business there will be a split between advisers, admin and paraplanners. Compliance, Finance & IT may be in-house or outsourced.

While I see many different models, and I will discuss the role of the paraplanner later, I would certainly say that any financial advice business wishing to scale must recognise the need to support financial planners with paraplanners and administrators as soon as possible if you want to avoid the financial advisers just becoming expensive administrators.

There are only 45 firms with more than 50 financial advisers and yet they employ 49% of the total authorised financial advisers in the market.

The smallest micro-business tends to have one financial adviser who is often the owner, backed up with an administrator. Compliance support is often outsourced and often two sole practitioners act as locum for each other.

47% of all the firms in the market only have one financial adviser. They often outsource their risk by being members of a network. It is all but impossible to scale this type of business as it's incredibly difficult for a sole practitioner to bring on more than one additional adviser without significantly cutting back his or her income.

The next level of advisory business has two to five authorised financial advisers. This is 42% of the firms in the market.

These firms often have an MD who also gives financial advice and leads a small team of financial advisers while an operations manager or director runs the back office and compliance.

Likewise, an effective financial advice business needs some form of business development if it is to grow in a planned way. In smaller businesses this is often the role for the MD, although my observation is that the current advice gap means most adviser firms have more than enough new client enquiries to live off, providing they have no ambition to grow exponentially.

Almost 90% of financial advice businesses have fewer than five financial advisers and have a relatively simple structure. They are not complex to run structurally, but like other professional practice businesses, that belies the challenges of operating as a regulated business in the first place.

The rise of the paraplanner

The paraplanner's role is a relatively recent addition to financial planning, having been introduced around the start of the 21st century.

In a short period, the role of the paraplanner has become paramount to successful financial planning businesses. A paraplanner's role is to take some of the administrative burden off a financial adviser but has expanded from its origins to incorporate research and report writing.

When paraplanners were first conceived, they were 'just' financial services administrators. Back in the early 2000s, as we've already established, financial advice was still a sales-led profession and reports were relatively straightforward. This gradually changed as regulation was introduced to the process, and since RDR this has accelerated.

With many more pressures on a financial planner to deliver high-quality, risk-rated advice and to ensure that the report and recommendations accurately meet a client's needs, the administrative and report writing burden has grown and grown... and grown.

The quality of and expectations on paraplanners have risen in line. Nowadays, most paraplanners are diploma qualified or similar, and there's been a big step up in the number of chartered paraplanners with level six or level seven qualifications.

Not surprisingly, salaries for financial paraplanners have risen significantly, as using a good paraplanner improves accuracy and efficiency. The paraplanner is no longer the poor relation of the financial planner, they just do a different job.

While a financial planner spends time in front of clients, paraplanners increasingly get involved in the fact-finding and advisory process, through reporting and even attending client meetings sometimes.

One big difference, however, is that the financial adviser is the person legally responsible for any advice given – even if someone else in the chain writes the recommendations. Responsibility for a mistake in any part of the process lies with the financial adviser.

While some paraplanners will go on to become full financial planners, the more flexible hours and less travel mean that many of the top paraplanners are careerists, earning significant salaries and making a major contribution to their company's success.

A good paraplanner will be highly technically competent and likely have an inquiring mind to solve problems, while the financial planner will increasingly focus their time on relationship building to help grow the firm – not in the old-fashioned way of persuading people to buy from them but in the modern way of building a trusted relationship over time with clients to help them in more wide-ranging ways and encouraging them to pass on referrals.

Paraplanning is now recognised as a profession in its own right, and a good paraplanner can really make a difference to a financial planning business, helping it provide an outstanding service to clients, or supporting financial planners, and helping the business to become even more efficient and more profitable.

There was a time when a team might have one paraplanner between four or five financial advisers, and often the paraplanner might be seen as only essential for major clients. Nowadays, however, a firm is more likely to want to ration the financial advisers' time, just focusing on the key interactions with clients – and as an adviser may, these days, have a bigger list of clients, they may have the support of a paraplanner and an administrator to divide the task into three.

It is possible to outsource paraplanning, as a paraplanner often does not need to meet the client. This makes the job attractive to people who might value the opportunity to work flexible hours from home.

Financial planning working with legal and accountancy practices

One of the really big changes since 2012 is the way that the legal and accounting professions regard financial planners and wealth managers.

Before 2012, a large part of the profession viewed financial planners with suspicion and, not surprisingly, many controlled the quality of financial advice their clients received by having their own financial planning practices. However, as the rules changed, most chose to close that aspect of their practice and instead act as introducers to IFAs and other financial planning businesses.

Whilst reforming the financial services industry with the Retail Distribution Review, the Government was also attempting a similar wholescale revamp of legal services. The idea was to open up the monopoly of solicitors, and thereby offer consumers alternative routes to accessing legal advice or services. This of course, was the concept for financial services with the RDR, but the legislation that was to shake up the law, at least in England and Wales, was the 2007 Legal Services Act. The Act came into full force in October 2011, but what did the legislation involve, and more importantly what would the changes mean for the legal profession, and for the financial advisers keen to work more closely with them?

The best person to ask was Dave Seager, a long-term industry friend and 13-years-in-position Director of SIFA (originally Solicitors for Independent Financial Advice). Dave retired from his final role as MD of SIFA Professional in 2021, but he is still a Consulting Adviser to the business, which since the early 1990s has worked tirelessly to increase true collaboration between the legal and financial advisory professions.

He said the role of SIFA had changed significantly since he joined their board in 2008.

"SIFA has always been nimble and quick to adapt its services as a result of changes in legislation and regulation, both in financial and legal services. Its raison d'etre has always been to encourage solicitors to recognise the frequent need for complementary financial planning in so many areas of the legal work they do. In the 1990s, as Solicitors for Independent Financial Advice (SIFA for short), this was by assisting law firms to get directly regulated for financial services, set up their own in-house IFA, and then ensure their compliance.

"At one point SIFA supported over 200 solicitor IFAs and at the peak, in England and Wales at least (as Scotland and NI have separate legal regulation), there were 750 of them. This represented about 10% of the solicitor population at the time, but the Financial Services and Markets Act, was to change things significantly and with it ultimately, SIFA's role."

Dave explained the reason why legislation addressing financial services so impactful on solicitors running in-house IFAs for their clients.

"The dawn of the FSA changed the regulatory landscape for in-house firms as the new regulator insisted that a partner/director of the solicitor firm had to fulfil the compliance function. Previously, whilst controlled solely by the Law Society, the in-house financial adviser, usually an employee of the law firm, could also be the Compliance Officer, but the FSA expected a senior lawyer to have final oversight. In short, the solicitors had not embraced financial services on these terms and were reluctant to have final sign-off on advice they did not feel qualified to understand. Therefore, from 2002, more and more of the 750 either hived off their financial services arm or closed them entirely. Today there are fewer than 50 directly (FCA) regulated solicitor firms."

Dave explained to me that SIFA gradually evolved, becoming more of a marketing and support provider to IFAs, seeking to work with the legal profession. The relationships built over a long period with the Law Society was still important but perhaps more so was the understanding of the changing legal services market and the changes that came with the Legal Services Act, and the new regulator it created. In 2008 SIFA launched SIFA

Professional solely to support advisers looking to build real relationships in the new world.

I asked Dave to outline what the changes were are why they were so significant?

> "Without going into the minutiae, the Act allowed external investment into solicitor firms, the ability for firms to allow non-solicitor management, and crucially separated the representative and regulatory function by creating the new Solicitors Regulation Authority (SRA). Before the Law Society fulfilled both roles, which in effect was akin to being the boss and the trade union. The Government was and is keen for the SRA to be a stronger regulator of the profession to ensure better outcomes for consumers, and it held up the FCA as a role model."

He explained that the Act also created a new style of business model, Alternative Business Structures (ABS) which were designed to offer flexibility for new and exciting consumer-centric firms, perhaps offering more than just legal services. These businesses have to have at least one solicitor in the management team and offer at least one 'Reserved Activity' such as conveyancing, litigation or grant of probate in addition to offering other services.

> He added "Such new ventures were allowed from October 2011, and one of the first SRA-authorised ABSs was Cooperative Legal Services. It remains one of the most successful new entrants, and along with others such as accountancy-owned legal firms Rocket Lawyer, Legal Zoom, and others, became strong – often cheaper than most commercially-minded alternatives to the high street solicitor."

He feels that this competition has increasingly led to sensible law firms considering a more commercial approach and importantly how to differentiate themselves from the traditional solicitor model.

> Dave explained that, "One obvious way to do so in my view, and in SIFA Professionals' back then, was for solicitors to re-embrace working with IFAs to provide a more complete and less commoditised proposition."

Dave continued, "There was a very clear steer in the first new SRA regulatory handbook in 2012, actually written by a senior ex-FSA figure, on the subject of third-party referral. In addition, the new rules created a new management compliance role within solicitor firms, the Compliance Officer for Legal Practice (COLP). This was thought to be a positive move as this individual was in theory responsible for ensuring that referrals to third parties from a firm of solicitors were in the client's best interests. The requirement to always act in the customer's best interests, however, was one of the principles included in the Solicitor's Code of Conduct.

"However, the due diligence, whilst suggested, to ensure a referral to a particular adviser, was in practice not properly overseen by the COLP. This is partly because the referral decision was in the individual code of conduct and COLPs could legitimately claim they trusted their staff to ensure best interests; but also because the rules were too long-winded, you all know about indicative behaviours and outcomes, and the SRA was likely to police the rules as, for example, the FCA would."

Happily, the SRA, under more focused management moved to simplify the rule book, from 400 plus pages to around 120, with a more concise set of principles and most significantly, for the first time in November 2019, adding a 'Firm Code of Conduct'. The COLP is now charged to create and implement proper firm-wide processes and systems for anything impacting the consumer, which of course should include how, why and to whom referrals are made at a firm level.

This should have, and increasingly has, removed the age-old problem of individual solicitors selecting their own personal favourite referees. Solicitor firms should have a panel or small list of carefully selected – based on real due diligence – financial adviser partners. The reason why the firm should include more than one financial planning partner, is that another of the SRA principles is to always act with independence, as well as in the client's best interests.

What should financial advisory firms be doing?

Dave feels that the key now, therefore, is to ensure a good understanding of the rules and to prepare an approach based on assisting the COLP with his or her due diligence. In short, make their role easier by demonstrating all the reasons why your firm is a safe pair of hands for their clients in terms of complementary financial advice. This might include your local reputation, your qualifications, your specialisms, how your advice and investment processes work, your fee structure, and how you can refer work back to them through the financial planning journey the clients will go on.

> He reminded me that this creates great opportunities for professional financial planners. "Now really is the time to press home how professional the top end of the financial planning industry has become. It coincides with a changing professional services world, post pandemic, where clients expect joined-up advice – where their needs and problems are not simple and encompass both legal and financial. As I always like to say, clients don't think in silos, so why offer them solutions in silos?"

Over the years, the relationship between Financial Planners and Professional Practice Firms has changed. Today, whether it is a legal firm or an accountancy firm referring the client, I suggest there is a mutual respect.

I work with many financial planning firms who work in this niche because it's a part of the market where the quality, experience and qualifications of a financial planner can be a key differentiator.

Financial Services Compensation Scheme (FSCS)

The financial services compensation scheme is the financial services industry's statutory compensation scheme for authorised financial services firms. It is free to all investors and paid for by the companies themselves. It pays compensation when a member firm is found liable by the FCA but is unable to pay. £26 billion has been paid out to 4.5 million people since it was set up.

While all firms must be happy that customers' compensation is guaranteed, there is a concern that the FCA decides who to authorise and monitors their compliance, but there is no come-back for members if the FCA is ineffective in its monitoring.

There is ongoing pressure from legislation. At present, the major controversy is the cost of the Scheme.

We've seen some bad (but not illegal) examples of 'phoenixing', where the directors closed a company down, walking away from their liabilities, and then opened another company the next day (or transfer their clients to another company they already own).

The FSCS then picks up these liabilities, and the whole industry foots the compensation bill if bad advice was given, while the owner/director sells on the valuable client relationships, realising the sale value of an asset with no liabilities. This cannot be in the interest of the industry as a whole.

It would appear that the regulator may have been caught napping, allowing phoenixing, without paying much attention. Many IFAs and others question why these 'bad apples' are allowed back into the industry, having often walked away from substantial liabilities.

We have seen some crazy examples where a business has grown quickly through taking some risks with its advice process, e.g., British Steel steelworkers advised to transfer their money out of their work pension scheme. Then, at the point where the business gets investigated by the regulator, the directors sell the company's clients to another entity while leaving the advice liability behind. The directors pick up a multi-million-pound paycheque, the company is wound up and compensation is effectively paid for by the rest of the industry (the ones who treated their clients correctly).

Whoever receives that bad advice needs to be compensated, but the idea that the people responsible for the bad advice can make significant profit from selling a non-encumbered client bank, which would otherwise have no, or even negative value, doesn't make sense.

I predict this will change as soon as the regulators get to grips with it. In the short term, the easiest way is to prevent directors of companies separating a company from its biggest asset (its clients), but in the longer term, a more sophisticated response will be needed.

What is to be done?

The larger financial advice companies understand that they need a three-prong strategy in order to succeed:

1. Acquire clients and maintain a long-term relationship with them;
2. Create and extend your client services/compelling client proposition;
3. Recruit skilled advisers/create a future generation of financial advisers.

If a business is to succeed in the future, it needs to plan the way it does these three things.

Of course, there is a core of self-employed financial planners who own substantial client banks. This was the battleground of the 1990s and the 2000s and even the 2010s as companies fought to attract these self-employed financial planners by paying a high percentage of commission and taking a small rake-off in exchange for little support. Today, this model is not coping well in the new highly regulated world.

The large networks are mainly losing money. In 2020, the FCAs latest returns show that the 45 largest firms (by number of financial advisers) had the lowest productivity and declared an average loss of £1M. This is presumably because their member firms are turning over too little and taking out too much!

We have already seen large players such as Intrinsic (owned by Quilters) culling some of its member firms on profitability grounds and raising fees for the rest.

Reshaping the business model

In an environment where there seems to be no quick fix to the number of authorised financial planners, which is leading to ever spiralling earnings, we are starting to see innovation in the structures and processes of some of the largest firms.

The obvious first move is for the profession to try to do more with less by changing the structure of a firm and the financial advice process.

Whereas the traditional model had a high number of self-employed financial planners largely driven by and rewarded for new business, we now see a model focused on client servicing and retention.

This ensures that firms can afford to invest in systems processes and staff. Changing the balance between sales and ongoing servicing naturally reduces costs and allows each financial adviser to look after more clients – perhaps reducing the need for 'hunter' financial planners, with more need for less costly administrators and paraplanners. Also, as businesses grow, business development, focused on client acquisition, will also become a separate function.

The work of an IFA business will become even more segmented. Administration, paraplanning and financial advice are already becoming separate parts of a combined process, but in future, even parts of financial advice could become more specialist. Will writing, protection and mortgage broking has already separated off, but we could certainly see some specialist financial areas segmented in the way that accountants run them.

Outsourced specialist technical help could become even more important to support the financial advice process and overstretched financial advisors. Just like a law firm consists of a number of specialists brought in to do different jobs, I could see the financial adviser fronting a business with access to different expertise behind the scenes – some internal and some outsourced.

Regulation

Financial advice firms will be more robust and the relationship with the regulator will change. The regulator will address the 'bad apples' in a more proactive way. However, good advisers will continue to cross-subsidise the bad ones.

With the increasing cost of regulation and PI cover as well as FSCS compensation rises leading to an increased advisor levy, many are choosing to move away from being directly authorised. There are horror stories of companies seeing 200+ % increases in their PI cost (if they can get it) and similar increases in the FSCS levy. So, it's not all roses in the garden, but for larger companies who see these costs as just part of the cost of business, they are able to scoop up the smaller-time advisers who can no longer justify being directly authorised.

Nowadays, these advisers have mainly made their choices. They may choose networks (who will increase their fees) or choose to be directly authorised, but increasingly they choose to sell their clients at the point of joining a firm (either for value today or a deferred buy-out). Companies don't just want the financial adviser's income today; they want his or her clients and the long trail of ongoing income that comes with them, and the advisers know it.

At present, the majority of regulator action is retrospective.

The regulator approves new members but does not approve advice, policies or products. If something goes wrong, it acts retrospectively to ban types of financial advice or products. It then takes action against the companies deemed to have given bad advice or disadvantaged customers. The FSCS pays out and money is collected. If the rogue firm closes down, it will not pay the compensation or fines, so the other members all pay via a levy.

Remarkably, the firm's owners often realise the value of their asset by either transferring the clients to another company or selling the unencumbered clients and pocketing the money while closing the company down and ending the liability.

This will end eventually but to date this practice continues. We must find a way of balancing regulatory & FSCS costs with business needs.

As I stated earlier in the book, regulation has driven significant numbers of advisers out of the market due to raising the barriers to entry, while at the same time increasing the value of the remaining financial planning practices and the salaries of those giving financial advice.

It has also professionalised the businesses by ensuring they have a more 'normal' look, i.e., a few financial planners and a significant back-office staff to process the work, protect the clients and ensure high quality financial advice can be given.

This means the companies are spending a higher amount of their income on providing a service to the end client rather than spending it all on 'sales'.

Of course, the relationship between the regulator and the financial planning firms will also change as they grow. It's already evident that the larger firms are in a much better position than smaller firms when it comes to dealing with the regulator. It could be argued that some of the bigger firms have been able to shape regulation to suit their purposes and undoubtedly the regulator has been reluctant to challenge the 'big guns'.

While no one would claim that the large firms have intentionally flouted the law, they are undoubtedly able to allocate more resources to news management and greater challenge to a regulatory investigation when it takes place. One can only surmise that the regulator knows their decision is more likely to be challenged by a big firm than a small firm and that may dissuade them from making marginal decisions.

Sharon Mattheus said this about repairing our reputation:

> "I think it's the industry, more than anything, that's had a bad reputation, and I think that is starting to change. Those guys who

were fly-by-nighters, I think we've got rid of all of those people, because – now it's hard work. It's not easy any more. So, it's those few people who are genuinely interested and wanting to help others, those of us that are still left behind.

"I think that, as an industry, we're really heading in the right direction, and I think people are starting to see us as professionals now. We're qualified, you can see we are, we've got certificates, and things to prove that we know what we're talking about.

"And I think because we're so highly regulated, people are feeling safer. There are not so many stories about – "Oh, I was ripped off, and somebody's gone and got their commission and I've lost all my money" – sort of thing. You don't really hear of that anymore."

Going back to clients, businesses can no longer rely on just new business. New advisers need clients and introducers. As companies become larger and more structured, they will identify new methods of client attraction and business development.

The need for financial advice will remain. There may be an advice gap and certainly any established financial adviser will readily say that there are plenty of people seeking financial advice so there is an imbalance at present. However, many people who want it may not be particularly profitable for a typical financial adviser. In Chapter 11, I will explain how Cameron Renton has needed to take on less profitable clients to get started.

Looking at the next generation (who will acquire or inherit wealth over the next 10–15 years), many of them have a different attitude to personal services.

- Young people don't trust financial advisers.
- Young people would prefer to do it themselves.
- Financial advisers are not retaining enough intergenerational relationships when wealth has cascaded down the generations.

Somehow, we need to recognise that the need for financial advice will continue to grow, but we don't always buy what we need, we buy what we want. Many of the Nextgen wealthy people may not recognise that they need financial advice, or at least, they will want to engage with financial advisers in a different way.

Range of services

The adviser firm of tomorrow is likely to offer a much wider range of services. We are already seeing the growth of life planning and the obvious add-ons such as mortgage and protection advice, general insurance and estate planning. However, there could be plenty of other areas to benefit.

At present, fully integrating financial advice, legal and accountancy is proving less attractive for professional advice firms such as solicitors and accountants than many might have expected a few years ago, partly due to the challenges of working with different regulators. As we have seen, there has been some contraction in that sector.

However, this is giving greater opportunity for cooperation between law firms and financial planning firms, with the growth of multi-service practices for both.

Although we have recently seen some new entrants who are committed to making it work, we remain acutely aware that regulation tends to slow innovation as companies put more money, time and effort into compliance than R&D. Nevertheless, Dave Seager argues this is merely the consequence of badly thought through regulation. It wasn't the intention and will probably be addressed at some stage.

Another key aspect will be the nature of client acquisition. Increased use of technology, perversely, has given the customer more choice but more confusion. Clients have become more likely to stay with the same firm, which is great for a business with enough existing clients, but in the long term, this will be a barrier to growth for many. There is an even greater need for businesses to create a trusted brand and find a way of engaging with new clients economically.

The Financial Adviser market will segment further, based on price and value

If we look at the American model, we can see that personal services such as top-end real estate, sales, and financial advice, become more highly-priced and less commoditized, while much of the back office work such as paraplanning, administration, and investment work can be done away from a central hub and often in far-off low cost economies.

There will be a rise in virtual advice, particularly for more transactional advice, but at the same time, the wealthier will value personal service even more greatly.

CHAPTER 8 SUMMARY

- The financial advice profession grew from protecting your family from eventualities to protecting and building wealth.

- Financial advisers are banding together to offer a wider range of services.

- The industry remains fragmented.

- The quality of financial advice has risen and the reputation of financial advisers is improving.

- The number of wealthy people is rising by five to seven per cent per year.

- Modern financial planning businesses are growing and less dependent on new business sales.

- Financial advisers can earn a good living from looking after their clients and earning ongoing fees.

- Since the start of the 21st century, paraplanners are becoming increasingly important.

- Accountants and solicitors increasingly view financial planners as their peers and are happy to refer clients.

- The law allows accountants, solicitors, and financial planners to have multi-disciplinary practices but the multitude of regulators makes this very difficult to operate in practice.

- The Financial Services Compensation Scheme offers great protection for clients

- The regulator needs to act faster and more effectively to prevent unsuitable practitioners from entering the market.

- If the regulator becomes more proactive, it will enhance the general public's view of the profession.

- Financial advice remains a 'people business'.

CHAPTER 9

The talent pool

According to a recent report by Octopus investments, 60% of financial planners turned away business in the past 12 months and this is predicted to get worse as 62% of the profession want to retire in the next 10 years. Not surprisingly, 67% of financial planners experienced difficulty finding talent. So, the 'advice gap' is very real and the industry needs to put time and effort into resolving this conundrum.

It has taken a long time to get here, but finally, after 30 years of declining financial adviser numbers, we appear to have reached the point where we need more advisers than we have.

The need for financial advice now is greater than it ever has been because of the complexities around taxation. And since RDR, the level of intervention of the state and the individual from a pension perspective, what we've just gone through this year will inherently change that. I have absolutely no doubt about that. So, the reliance upon private provision or personal provision is going to be hugely increased moving forward.

The advice gap is still growing which Cameron Renton knows, means great opportunities for advisers.

"People will still buy and sell houses. So, there's work there for mortgage advisers. People still need protecting so there is a need for protection advisers. I think the need for pension provision at the

moment is great, greater than it probably ever has been because there is a generation coming along now who may not get much in terms of a state provision. So, for me, I think there's more opportunity than ever at the moment, certainly in the industry."

However, the challenges are many.

- More are leaving than joining the profession.
- Not enough young people generally are interested in becoming financial advisers.
- Not enough women are choosing to join the profession.
- The current financial model for new financial advisers means it's hard to earn while you learn.
- Some of the companies that offer training for their financial advisers are struggling to make the advisers profitable once they have been trained.
- Training the next generation.

It's clear at this point that people are not lining up to join the ranks of the profession.

Furthermore, as we have seen, the current financial model for new entrants is still largely broken. As I mentioned earlier, with 90% of UK financial advice businesses having five or fewer authorised financial advisers, and some of the largest players still using a self-employed model, they are not really in a position to fund the type of training costs required to bring on and train new financial planners.

Change in the financial adviser demographic

Not only are we failing to attract new advisers, but we also have an aging population of current advisers, caused by 30 years' decline. There is an anomaly in the financial adviser demographic which I would argue has been caused by legislation and the way it has been enacted up to this point.

Back in the 1960s to late 1980s, we have seen there were no significant barriers to entry to being a financial adviser. Qualification requirements were low or non-existent, and commission levels were high so even a new financial adviser with good prospecting skills could earn well quite quickly. As legislation started to bite and the banks started to take a big chunk of the market, barriers to entry rose and individual advisers found it more difficult to prospect for clients, while banks, who had access to mass affluent clients, tended to keep most of the commission they earned for themselves.

The result was that fewer people were attracted to the adviser profession.

Compliance also meant the role became more administrative, so there was a change in the type of person who chose to be a financial adviser, from entrepreneurial to more administrative with greater attention to detail, and often more interest in the technical aspects of financial advice.

Under the old commission system, it was possible to earn a reasonable living from a few new business cases, but the downside was that the salesman was only as good as his or her last sale.

In more recent years, companies began a long, slow transition towards ongoing fees.

Initially, and well before RDR, we started to see a small amount of trail commission on investment bonds (perhaps 0.25%) in addition to the traditional initial commission but as the industry moved towards fees and away from initial commission, we started to see many advisor businesses adopt a model which looks more familiar today.

These financial advisers were not replaced for many years, meaning a significant proportion of regulated financial advisers are in the 50+ age range and a relatively low number are younger.

Addressing the gender gap

Financial advice, like many other professions, has always been predominantly male. Despite considerable progress being made in large companies such as asset managers and product providers, women only make up 17% of approved FCA individuals. This percentage has hardly changed since 2005.

It's estimated that in the UK as a whole, £150 billion in additional GDP could be generated by closing the gender gap by 2025 (McKinsey Global Institute 2016, 'The power of parity: Advancing women's equality in the United Kingdom').

Although men continue to dominate the highest paid roles and work in the highest paid sectors, there is much more recognition of this inequality, and a lot more has been addressed.

Now that larger companies are forced to disclose their gender gap figures with the result that we now know the median pay gap across the economy is 18% in favour of men. Just one in 10 executive positions in FTSE 100 companies are held by women, and over 80% of large employers have more women in their lowest paid positions than their highest paid positions.

While there are many reasons for this, there is no doubt that financial services could be seen as slow to the party, but are now catching up fast.

Large companies have led the way in financial services, and we are now beginning to see quite a high number of women reaching the highest levels in the profession. Recent announcements within FTSE companies such as Quilter, St James's Place and others, show companies are actively encouraging women and a higher percentage of women are now reaching MD level and beyond.

Gillian Hepburn is a leading member of the Women in Platforms group, a networking group for women in the investment platform industry. Having spent three decades in close contact with IFAs, Gillian is well aware of the traditional evening work associated with the financial planning profession and said that wasn't necessarily helpful for women.

> "Going back to the days of Allied Dunbar through to the early brokers, some might feel it wasn't a particularly female friendly job. Financial advice was often an evening profession and it's going to take a generation for that change. When we did all the work with advisers, post RDR, charging fees for service and changing your business

model, we talked a lot about the fact that the adviser profession was visiting people at unsociable times. So, women with small children were unable to go out at six o'clock, but that's when clients want to meet you. When they are at work, they don't have time to do it."

Nowadays, you are much more likely to come across high powered women such as Gillian within financial services than used to be the case, but there is still a gender imbalance, and this is most evident in the financial adviser ranks.

Louise Hunt started in banking and told me:

"What you'll find in financial services is that lot of support staff are female. Very few support staff are male. So being a financial adviser is not seen as a female role. I think that's because of gender stereotypes when we were growing up.

"Is it nature or nurture? Do girls naturally get drawn to wanting to be a hairdresser or a makeup artist or that kind of role, rather than finance?... because it's not that sexy, is it? It's quite a challenging environment.

"But I think those who are passionate about people should be driven towards it. Those who really want to help people. It should be seen as the fifth emergency service, alongside your ambulance, your air, your fire, that kind of stuff. We are there to look after their financial health and I think that's overlooked a lot.

"And I think men were maybe driven down that route more, even if they weren't very good at it. Sometimes it was just because banking was seen as a man's job."

Just like Gillian, Louise also referred back to history.

"My mum told me that in the seventies you couldn't be married as a woman and work in a bank. You were told the minute you got married, you had to hand in your notice. Back then, women were only just getting that equality. But some women didn't believe they could

earn that kind of money. And they were actually told, "You can't have that job because you're a woman."

But now, Louise feels her generation of women, whose mums saw that situation change, are no longer accepting of this status quo. However, financial advice may not seem a logical career so they need role models to make them believe it can be an attractive choice for them. Louise certainly feels the weight of responsibility to encourage the next generation of women to consider financial advice as a profession.

"As a female line manager, I really encourage the women that I work with to be the best. Because I do feel that as a woman, you need to prove yourself more than a man, in this environment. And in most, if I'm honest. If you want to be a successful woman, you do have to work harder than a guy."

One such woman is Sharon Mattheus. Brought up in South Africa, Sharon moved to the UK with her husband and young family before moving into financial services. She started as an administrator/paraplanner before taking the plunge and working through Foster Denovo as a self-employed financial planner.

Although she was successful, like many men and women before her the lack of security with being self-employed was one of the less attractive aspects of the profession.

Now she is a financial planner for Lovewell Blake, the IFA arm of a major accountancy business based in Bury St Edmunds, advising high net worth clients and company directors. The work is interesting and more complex, and Sharon appreciates the security of an employed role.

Sharon is a winner of numerous awards and has demonstrated she can compete successfully in a male dominated profession and is modest about how she overcame challenges along the way.

"Traditionally it's very much a male-dominated world. I think that back in the day, it might have been that you had to do a lot of socialising, and when you're working in this industry, it was all about

getting together and doing those kind of social networking events, and that sort of thing."

Sharon identified laddish culture and socializing to be issues which may have put women off the profession in the past.

"I think as a woman, you've got to be a little bit careful and cautious about how you do that. A group of guys going out and drinking and that sort of thing is acceptable. A group of guys with one woman is not quite so acceptable. And honestly, I don't think I'd be comfortable in that kind of situation."

But it's not only the socializing aspects which deterred a lot of women. Personal safety is another area of concern to some.

"Advisers go to a client's home, because that's where a client's comfortable, and everything's there. So, when you get there, if you need anything, it's to hand, and they're in their comfort zone. I've done a number of evening appointments."

Sharon recognises the fear factor but reminded me that her own South African upbringing may make her braver than some!

"I can't say that I've ever felt uncomfortable, but then I am from South Africa! I think you've just got to be sensible whoever you are, and we've got our electronic diaries, so people know where I am, that sort of thing."

What does Sharon believe is the secret to her success? She told me:

"Probably the fact that I've dealt with a lot of different people helps me to adjust to individuals when I see them. So, I can be comfortable with a very wealthy person just as easily as somebody who says: 'This £10,000 is going to be my lifeline, what do I do with it?' So, I can adjust. And I think it's more the type of person you are than your experiences, almost. I'm good at adjusting to anybody. I can get on with anybody, and my skill, I feel, one of my strengths is to just really be able to get information without trying!"

The issues of self-employment, laddish culture and personal safety are all issues she recognises might put many women off, although she has dealt with them with aplomb.

Gillian acknowledges the career support she received from Standard Life.

"I moved every two years, I moved to different roles. I had a really exciting time. I had lots of opportunities. I never ever felt, ever, that I was held back because I was a woman. They did things like sponsoring my MBA."

So, Gillian made progress in a company who appeared to be actively encouraging women to progress into management and she didn't really think about the fact that this was not the norm elsewhere. The first time she realised it wasn't normal was when she moved into sales and distribution, a part of the company which was really male dominated.

"Suddenly, as a woman, I was in the absolute minority. I started as a national development manager for product launch and development work focused on marketing. I wasn't actually out selling until a few years later. Although it felt quite male dominated, the person that moved me to sales was a woman. She was the Head of Strategy and Ops and... and the team was mixed, there were four senior managers, two men, two women. So again, gender wasn't an issue but obviously what I suddenly realised was that the sales team of what we now call BDMs were predominantly male. Out of 300 in broker development there were no female branch managers, one national account manager and the two of us in strategy. That was it."

Gillian used this to her advantage. The IFAs were not used to women calling on them.

"Suddenly they (IFAs) have got this female coming to their door that doesn't necessarily want to talk about football and stuff. Although I was always happy to have a chat, I talked about things they wanted to talk about because that's what you do in sales, and I had two small children at the time. They quite liked the child talk and actually identified with that."

She recognised that being a woman helped her stand out from all her male competitors. I asked Gillian if she experienced any actual prejudice against women at that time?

"Not personally, no, I didn't feel it. You deal with people who like you and you get on with. I pretty much get on with anybody."

Of course, she did experience old fashioned views at times.

"Some men had this perception that they didn't necessarily want to deal with women. I remember getting on a flight once, the red eye from Edinburgh. It was my first business trip. I was really super excited. I was going to Plymouth. I was still on the management training scheme, so I was probably about 22 or 23. So, I bought a new suit to fly. How excited I was. So, I arrived at Plymouth Airport, and the branch manager 'collected me' at the airport, and he took one look at me, and he said, 'I just need to tell you that I do not approve of women wearing trousers to work.'

"This was 1990. He was in his late fifties, male & pale. He probably didn't approve of women working full stop, but the trousers were just too much!

"So, he put me on the back foot. He just laughed. He clearly had a prejudice. And that was the first time I kind of thought, 'well, he's got an interesting view on women!' But I didn't really take it personally."

Louise's comments were a little stronger.

"Honestly, I would say you have to have a thick skin. It's a very male-driven environment. And when you're in that kind of environment, you get a lot of egos. So, you have to be able to have confidence and belief in yourself."

I asked Gillian about extra challenges. What challenges did she face?

"I absolutely am an advocate of diversity, and having diversity of thought as well as gender. I think that's important as well as you've got to have the right women there.

"If you have a family, sadly there has to be some sacrifices in a way, but it's about how you manage it. As a woman with small children, there were late nights and there were very early mornings in terms of getting in the car, driving off somewhere, hold-ups and delays and missing flights to London.

"There's a statistic that women typically either leave industry or their career kind of stops at age 38. I don't know the reasons but maybe, for most women, if they've got kids, and young people are having their children later and later all the time, their children are probably really young at the height of their career, when they're still at school and they need you. Yeah. So, I'm not saying that's the case for everybody, but it's a challenge."

I then asked Gillian Hepburn about the opportunities for women within the profession.

"Actually, for me, financial planning massively plays into women's strengths because it's all about managing relationships with clients. It's not about selling products anymore.

"Over the 30 years I've been in the industry, it's all about helping people understand what their financial goals are and how they're going to get there. And if they're going to get there and if not, what we can do to help. Yes. And, and, and you would, you would almost assume that that plays much more naturally to women's strengths.

"I think when women are more curious, they're a bit more open. They're happy. I think to have some of what can be some of these more challenging conversations we just don't talk about cold cash. I think many women they would find it rewarding."

The importance of quality people and of building a trusted brand

While we've undoubtedly seen the rise of virtual banking and virtual financial advice, people still want brands and names they can trust. We've certainly seen that challenge banks who have not risen as fast as they might, and that undoubtedly demonstrates the value of having a good brand behind you.

Guardian 1821 Group is a case in point. The directors of the company (which was in fact, a start-up) had previously built another company (Bright Grey) from zero. They've realised the value of a known brand and purchased the Guardian brand from Resolution Group, who bought the remnants of Guardian Royal Exchange and its sub-brands a few years before.

In the case of a financial planner, there are very few trusted brands. Most small businesses have historically relied on word of mouth and recommendation. if you've never had advice and you have a large lump sum (£250,000 pounds plus) to invest for the first time, you probably want to meet a real person, and probably not just online where it's hardest to build up trust.

Trust is still at the core of Financial Planning but it's the personal touch and not branding which is seen as core by many. Some of our largest companies including St James's Place, Quilter, Charles Stanley and Close Brothers who all focus on wealth management, seem to value their brand, which is often used across various businesses. However, others seem to be creating new names with no heritage such as Amber River, Evelyn Partners and others.

Millennials have much more trust in online, and the millennials are gradually inheriting the money. However, at the present time, it's the baby boomers, born between 1946 and 1964, who hold the majority of the private wealth (often in the form of pensions), and their trust in online investing is less.

Of course, trust is not just about brand. It is also about people. Before finalising this book, I gave Cameron Renton, an Edinburgh based financial adviser and sole trader, a call and he told me that he recently had the opportunity to buy a small book of clients from a retiring IFA in the north of Scotland. He told me that the vendor had several potential buyers who were prepared to pay more than he was, but he sold the client bank to Cameron because he trusted him to treat his clients right. Cameron is based in the Scottish central belt and was willing to commit to face-to-face review meetings with the Aberdeen-based clients at least annually and the retiring adviser said he wanted to be certain that his clients were entrusted to a financial adviser who would look after them. In this case, Cameron himself was the trusted brand.

Addressing the shortage of financial advisers – who pays for training?

It will take a long time to address the financial planner shortage. Solutions still need to be found to grow the number of financial advisers in the market.

It is many years since there has been such an opportunity available to the financial advice profession, but we need to attract different people to those we did in the past.

I will touch on training in the next chapter, although it's relevant here as well. Even though the industry has a shortage of financial advisers, most of the medium and small advice firms are too small to fund their own graduate schemes. A new unqualified or recently qualified financial adviser will not become profitable for a considerable time if they have to build their own client bank, so the acquisitive businesses have a model which relies on planned growth.

Usually a Private Equity (PE) House will seek to own a business for a fixed period, maybe 7 years, while seeing spectacular growth. With this in mind, a consolidator business needs to acquire business and client banks efficiently, either running a hub-and-spoke model or an integrated model. In either case, the trick it needs to achieve is to acquire relevant skills in line with its acquisitions.

Usually when a business is acquired, some of the business owners/ principals will retire and will need to be replaced by an employed adviser to take over and manage the client bank. It will also be necessary to have operational staff and compliance staff to manage client transition as clients lost in transit will reduce its value.

Investors are seeking a quick return so a Private Equity House with a 5-to-7-year plan is not going to be willing to invest in anything which is unlikely to yield a profit in that timescale. They don't want trainees. They want fully trained, experienced financial advisers who can operate at pace from day one.

Back in the days of bancassurance, moving from banking to a career in financial advice was common. Louise Hunt explains:

"It was usually a support member of staff that'd be seen to be really good, who would be really passionate about clients and who would then start developing themselves prior to getting on any scheme or any programme. They would start taking the exams and show an interest in the role because they liked what they saw. They wanted to better themselves and develop themselves. So sometimes it would be a referral from an advisor saying that someone working in the branch is doing a brilliant job. I think that'd be really good as an advisor. Then we would sit down and have a chat with them as a manager and say yes or no, and then put them on the trainee scheme."

With the demise of bancassurance I asked her how easy it is to become a financial planner today?

"I think it's harder. There are trainee financial planning roles still out there. I think people used to go self-employed as a financial adviser more in the past because you could make more money. Fundamentally, it was easier to make money and you had very little regulation. And if you think back to the '90s, you only had to take three exams. It was dead easy. Then it got more and more complicated, with more exams. So, more and more people have left the market than are joining. I think that's going to be a big problem.

"I don't think it's as easy to get into financial planning. And I don't think it's seen as sexy for the younger people today either. They want to get into social media, they want to be an influencer, so they don't want to have to work hard for it. "Let me be a footballer or something like that, or just be on Tiktok and earn money through people watching my videos!"

One model is for small financial planning firms to train and promote from within. Developing their own staff to gradually take over as financial advisers, but this also may not fully address the skills gap.

Figures from the FCA suggest there is still a shrinking talent pool of financial planners. In the end, this will need to be addressed.

Adapting business models to address the adviser shortage

Some wealth firms seem to be changing their structure, to look more like other professions, ensuring a relatively small number of authorised financial advisers are kept extremely busy and are supported by an extensive back-room team.

Darren Smith gave me his views.

> "I learnt early on in my career that, if you make the adviser have more time, he or she can do what he or she does best, which is to go and see clients. So actually, some of the most successful businesses that I came across, where you might only have two or three advisers, but you'd have a back office of 10 or 12 people. And the advisers were just out constantly seeing clients, simple business. The servicing could all be done by someone junior back in the office.

> "The junior talks to the client, collects a whole lot of information and organises for the financial adviser to meet the client, maybe to do a top-up or something and then immediately hands it back to the administrator back in the office, but that doesn't increase the number of advisers."

So, by using less qualified back office staff to take on some non-regulated tasks, making the financial advisers' use of time more efficient, wealth businesses can ensure economies of scale without reducing the service.

However, while this can reduce the number of financial advisers required to fill the advice gap, it's pretty clear we are still way short of that number.

As we see more, and larger, firms, there is more opportunity to create efficiency. They might be able to have a small number of business developers who bring in business deals and introducer arrangements to the team.

There is some anecdotal evidence that the shortage of financial advisers is leading to some more innovative thinking in the mid-size firms. I have seen a number of mid-sized industry firms start to find ways of developing their own financial advisers as well as poaching advisory talent from their competitors.

I am also aware that a number of new entrants are driving the salaries of advisers even higher. In the medium term, even these so called 'consolidators' will find that the shortage of available financial advisers may limit their ability to grow.

Darren mentioned to me that, in his opinion, there are loads of acquirers out there at the moment but there aren't enough who are generating new blood. As adviser businesses are starting to become more attractive, so prices are rising in terms of the income multiples.

"If we were to look at the 'sub' top 50 firms, those who now have 10 or so advisers now and had maybe five advisers six years ago, we can see how quickly they've grown by being willing to invest in their own businesses and acquire other businesses in the sector."

He went on to explain that these businesses often have a fairly young, entrepreneurial business owner who knows that they can sell their business by gaining scale quickly.

"I have seen smaller firms who are trying to scale up but finding it difficult to bring in new financial planners".

We all recognise that young entrepreneurs have a unique approach to problem solving which may eventually lead to innovative approaches not even thought of today.

So maybe, with the shortage of financial planners creating barriers to their companies growing, we will see young ambitious business owners create some innovative ways to bring in new blood and train in a cost-effective way.

The work of an IFA business will become even more segmented. Administration, paraplanning and financial advice are already becoming separate parts of a combined proess, but in future, even parts of financial advice could become more specialist. Not only will protection/mortgage broking have already separated off but we could certainly see some specialist financial areas segmented in the way that accountants run them.

Outsourced specialist technical help could become even more important to support the financial advice process and the overstretched financial advisors. Just like a law firm consists of a number of specialists brought in to do different jobs, I could see the financial adviser fronting a business with access to plenty of different expertise behind the scenes, some internal and some outsourced.

New roles

The role of the business development manager within financial advice firms will grow.

A few years ago, most business development managers worked within the product providers and the key task was to face into the adviser community, persuading them that they had the best product or solution. Today, the providers, asset managers, discretionary fund managers and life companies all have a small number of specialist, highly skilled business development managers who provide specialist support only to their key supporters, ignoring the wider market and enabling firms to grow the new business from existing IFAs and advice firms.

However, the demise of the BDM within the product providers has benefited many of the larger advice firms who've been able to hire really good relationship managers to help build third party relationships with introducers. Increasingly, the role of the sales managers is not the Training and Competence (T&C) function (which is carried out by another) but is actually the business development function, not only supporting advisers with their everyday needs, but also helping them to develop external connections who can introduce business to the practice.

CHAPTER 9 SUMMARY

- The need for financial advice now is greater than it's ever been.

- The advice gap is growing, the demand for financial advice is growing, the supply of financial advisers is shrinking.

- Many financial advisers are at or close to retirement.

- More advisers are leaving the talent pool than joining it.

- Financial advice is a male-dominated profession. Women only make up 17% of approved FCA individuals, and there has been no real change in the past few years.

- Women may be suited to the profession, but the profession has done little thus far to get its message out to them.

- The shortage of financial advisers needs to be addressed.

- The traditional routes for training advisers are largely closed to new entrants.

- Some financial client practices are adapting their business models to address the adviser shortage.

- As firms grow, they will separate business development from financial advice, and start to attract business development managers from the product providers.

CHAPTER 10

Attracting and training the next generation

As I write this in March 2022, there are approximately 27,500 financial advisers who are authorised to give investment advice in the UK.

It is estimated that 15,600 or so financial advisers will leave the profession in the next 10 years, so with natural turnover in addition, we probably need to bring in at least 2,000 new financial advisers per annum just to stand still. The four highest profile financial adviser schools are St James's Place, Quilter, The Openwork Partnership and SimplyBiz. They currently bring in around 700 new financial advisers per annum and even though there are a few smaller training opportunities, the shortfall is considerable.

We know that a significant proportion of the current adviser crop either entered the industry as self-employed financial advisers, through one of the large direct salesforces when barriers to entry were low and commissions were high, or through the bancassurance route where training was provided and most clients were transactional, generated by referral from an extensive bank branch network.

The industry now faces a much bigger challenge. Barriers to entry in the form of exams are high and initial investment fee income is very low. Cameron and Darren have both mentioned the need to supplement earnings from other sources such as mortgage and protection commissions for financial advisers when just starting out.

If we are to increase the number of advisers, we need to find a way of bringing in new blood. In this chapter I look at what the industry is doing now to address this and what more can be done in the future.

Persuading new entrants to join the profession

Despite the fact that demand for financial advice exceeds supply, there is more work to be done. Most people know very little about it. Only a small percentage of the population can afford it, which means most young people will never consider it as a profession.

Financial planning can be a great career, but not enough people know it according to Gillian Hepburn. She said to me:

> "I'm always an optimist and I think what we just have to be sure is that right back at school, university, wherever, is that people start to think about careers, that they haven't got a bias against becoming a financial adviser. It's not just men in suits and you don't have to be really good at economics or maths. It's about genuinely helping people.
>
> "It's a combination of coaching and being a bit of a social worker, and just having some really interesting conversations with clients and then taking that and helping them. We always still have to remember that we are a regulated business. So, it's a privilege to manage somebody's money, somebody's hard-earned cash."

Mergers and acquisitions are creating an opportunity for the next generation of financial advisers to join organisations with professional structures and strong client banks. Most importantly, the fact that wealthy clients now provide ongoing revenue for financial advisers makes them more attractive to other financial advisers in the event of advice businesses discontinuing.

Becoming more inclusive

The Equality Act of 2010 makes it clear that employees, workers and candidates looking for work, and the general public, are entitled to protection. The list of what this protection covers has become longer over the years with sexual orientation being the latest. The purpose of the Act is to protect people in each of the relevant groups, however, regardless of whether an Act is place, a diverse workforce is good for a business.

The purpose of the Equality Act is obviously to make things equal in employment and other matters across the board, but this necessarily takes time. The Recruitment & Employment Confederation, the leading recruitment trade body, promotes high standards in recruitment.

According to the REC website, a recent review into race in the workplace by RNS McGregor Smith and a review into ethnic diversity on boards by Sir John Parker stated that:

1. The employment rate for ethnic minorities is only 62.8% compared with the employment rate for white workers of 72.6% -a gap of over 12 percentage points;
2. All BME groups are more likely to be overqualified than white ethnic groups, but white employees are more likely to be promoted than all other groups;
3. 53 of the FTSE 100 companies do not have any directors from a BME background.

The FCA does not currently publish data on ethnicity, so it is difficult to comment on the current ethnic diversity. I'm sure the FCA will issue appropriate data in the future.

Many of my company's clients actively encourage us to seek out female talent and often request gender-balanced shortlists, but we are still some way from achieving parity.

I talked to Gillian Hepburn about this. Gillian grew up in Scotland, gained an English degree and intended to become an English Teacher, but, after a week's work experience in a school persuaded her that teaching was not for her, she joined Standard Life following a suggestion by her next-door neighbour who was head of HR. Gillian is now the UK intermediary solutions director at Schroders.

> "I got in on their graduate training scheme. It was the first year they had ever had women on their graduate management scheme because up until that point, the only training scheme was for actuaries, which was clearly a male dominated game for people with maths or similar degrees.

> "I never even thought that was a gender issue. The scheme consisted of four women and no men! "It's all different now, but financial advice was often an evening profession. And I think post RDR, we started to question, "Why are you getting in a car and driving 15 miles to have a cup of tea with somebody at seven o'clock at night and then drive back again?"

She now thinks there are more opportunities for female financial advisers in the future.

> "And now maybe this new (post COVID) environment will change that. You can book a call at any time. I've been hearing examples that in the era of zoom calls advisers are finding it easier to get men and women, husbands and wives on the call because we don't want to be going into people's houses any longer."

Gillian thinks the increased use of technology may be part of the answer.

> "If you look at that business model and the profitability of it, what you need to be doing is getting them to come and see you. But while travelling to you is great in terms of adviser profitability, as a client, "It's not for me. I want to meet you when it suits me, not when it suits you". So, I think things are changing. And you do wonder if the rise in technology will help women, in particular as it will mean that we do have different ways of dealing with customers going forward."

Sharon Mattheus also sees things changing for the better.

"I think women are starting to think about becoming financial advisers now. I've got a paraplanner who would love to be an adviser. It will be hard for her, but I will encourage her to make the change. I would just say, as a woman, believe in yourself, don't listen to what they're telling you. You've got this far, and there's a reason why you've got here."

Louise also said:

"Challenges for women within themselves, is seeing the opportunity and, obviously, the interest to go into it. And once you're into it there is a good opportunity for you to progress through it. I'm hoping the way that children are being brought up today, in a very gender-neutral environment, means there's more belief that you can be anything you want to be in this day and age."

So, are things changing already?

Julian Hince, Director of the Quilter Financial Adviser School, thinks they are. He told me there's no shortage of applicants, male or female. Whereas only 17% of the full financial adviser population is female, 32% of the people going through the adviser school are women. Julian said that the historic figures are skewing the percentages. 10% of advisers over 50 are women whereas 30% of advisers under 45 are women, so the problem may be less about the profession's ability to attract women than it is its ability to appeal to all young people.

Promoting financial advice as a profession to attract university and school leavers

There is still an important issue in raising the profile of financial advice, and in particular, making it a considered career choice for young people.

Cameron told me that he thinks we are living in possibly one of the greatest ever times for the financial advice sector providing people are willing to look at it as an opportunity.

"We've got an opportunity now to re-engage with people who we've not engaged with for a while. I think there are real opportunities if you are willing to shrug off the sort of old school mentality, if you want to call it that, and really get back to basics of just giving good advice to people who need that.

"There are a lot of positives at the moment. Even when you look at it in terms of income, I see more opportunities than threats. You just have to look around you."

The opportunity for people entering the profession is massive. We just need to get the message right.

I asked Darren if he had any suggestions about how the industry can address the financial adviser shortage and declining numbers. In particular, what about an apprentice scheme through further education colleges?

"I don't think it will gain enough traction through colleges. The one thing that they lack is they are educational experts. They're not industry experts."

Most agree that being a financial adviser is not yet seen as equal to solicitor, accountant or doctor when someone is considering careers from school. The industry has yet to engage in a meaningful way with schools and universities.

Julian Hince recognises the need for this to change. He is passionate about financial advice and feels that financial adviser profession suits the desires of many young people who want: "variety, flexibility and the opportunity to meet people". The financial advice role meets all of this. When I spoke to him, he told me he would be speaking to 100 14-year-olds at a school the following week.

Attracting career switchers

In the case of Quilter Adviser School, once he had proof of concept, Darren said they focused on bringing in non-traditional second careerists with connections and life experience. He said:

"We could bring something to the marketplace that really attracts the new, new blood."

Darren said that he initially spent a lot of time out in universities and colleges doing promotions and marketing and attracting young people, but he also identified the opportunity to attract career changers.

"We signed the armed forces covenant so we could engage some ex-forces personnel, and we supported women returners. So basically, we were striking deals with organisations way outside of the financial services sector to promote what we were doing. We built a structure that would allow firms to take somebody into their business as a trainee; might even be a trainee working in administration. So, they're doing some work to help the firm whilst getting the necessary qualifications."

Quilter has taken individuals from businesses such as Middlesex Country Cricket Club and the Army to encourage people to transfer over as a second career. Before the COVID-19 pandemic, Quilter introduced a fast-track scheme, which could get people to level four in three months on a full-time course. This works very well with the Army in particular, as they give their leavers three months' paid time to find a new career. Julian said it's been particularly effective with them, and they often have the right skillset, which can be transferable.

Attracting other new entrants

We have looked at second careerists and graduates. While big product providers like M&G Investments, St James's Place and Quilter have adviser academies and schools, very few others appear to be investing in trainees. A few are investing in upgrading to level six qualifications.

However, there is an obvious source of talent which is not yet being fully exploited. Internal talent.

Sean told me, "I think a lot of the best future advice talent probably is already within the industry.

It might be sitting in Cirencester (Head Office). It might be sitting in some of our locations. It is almost definitely sitting within the support staff functions of all of the partner businesses we've got. We've got a population of 6,000 odd support and there is so much latent talent in there."

Creating a pathway for new advisers

Very few financial advice firms have the finance and infrastructure to offer a financial adviser training scheme. Even some of the largest, who have the funding and scale, do not have an interest in offering it due to short-term goals.

Today, for an individual wishing to enter the financial advice profession, barriers to entry are high, and training is expensive and not usually fully funded. The traditional entry route is now largely outdated so a few small financial advice businesses might occasionally train a valued member of their administration staff to become an adviser, but this is relatively rare.

The slightly larger, more ambitious companies tend to be in a hurry. They prefer to recruit a proven adviser than to train their own. Until quite recently they would poach from their local competitors and hope that the adviser could bring some clients with them to cover their salary costs.

However, as the value of financial advice businesses have risen, they have sought to protect their client banks by writing non-compete or non-deal clauses into their financial adviser contracts, so this approach rarely works now.

All this means that only businesses with clients or a ready supply of high-quality leads can afford to bring in financial advisers -and they don't want trainees or newly qualified advisers; they want high-quality proven advisers who are used to dealing with wealthy clients and will be instantly trusted by their clients.

They have no interest in developing their own. They want instant results, so they poach from competitors. That's great for specialist head hunters like my company, so I am not complaining, but it doesn't bring in any much-needed new blood.

So only the largest companies with long-term intentions are willing to 'grow their own financial advisers'. With this in mind, we need to look at the few firms that have the scale and ability to develop their own.

The financial adviser schools and academies

I have mentioned a few times about the financial adviser academies. Four of the largest financial advice companies have their own academies.

1. St James's Place, who currently has 200 graduating per annum.
2. Quilter Financial Advice School, which had 300 graduating per annum but has now scaled back to 50 per annum.
3. SimplyBiz Academy, which has between 85 and 100 graduating per annum.
4. Openwork Academy, which has around 85 to 100 graduating per annum.

Creating a successful business model for a financial adviser school

Darren Smith took on the Quilter Financial Advisor School (FAS) when Intrinsic Network bought it from Sesame Bankhall Group. Intrinsic Network then rebranded to become part of Quilter.

Darren started his financial services career as a self-employed financial adviser before spending time as an employed financial planner and a compliance professional. When he had a family, he chose to become an employed financial adviser at Eagle Star until they closed the employed business down.

After several other roles Darren found himself at Intrinsic when they purchased Sesame Bankhall's financial adviser school. The business was making a loss at the time and also had a very low success rate with graduates. He was asked if he could turn it from a liability to an asset for the group by improving the pass rates and getting it to break even.

Improving examination success rates

Darren explained how he achieved this:

> "I realised only 50% graduated because a whole load of students who had failed exams along the routes were never given the opportunity to go back through FAS to re-study or redo the exam other than the immediate re-sit."

Darren spoke to some of the successful students, and they explained which parts they found most difficult. Darren quickly realised that the exams the adviser school team were failing were the highly technical, specialist exams with scenarios that even an experienced financial adviser might very rarely deal with.

Anyone who has ever studied for professional exams will, I am sure, find this resonates with them.

> "I have taken quite a few industry exams in my time and yet the practical application at any point in time within the job can be fairly minimal. If you're a career changer, the likelihood is you won't have done exams for 10, 20 years. And we know that doing an exam is often more about technique than it is actually about knowledge. So, the CII route to me was a very academic route."

Darren decided to identify a more appropriate (ideally more practical) course.

"I then looked at the London Institute of Banking and Finance (LIBF), which is far more of a practical route. They had a level 4 equivalent called DipFA which started with the module Financial Services, Regulation and Ethics (FSRE). It's a pretty tough exam, but then after that, everything becomes practical. So, you do a case study and the case study is an assessment and the final exam is actually a fact-find; it's proper fact-find. It's exactly like doing the job."

Darren said that he realised there is a lot of industry snobbery about CII being the gold standard qualification but once he sat and spoke to established Financial Planners about it, they all agreed that "once you've done it, and you are level four qualified, no-one really cares which route you took".

He then discussed the practical aspects of academic route (CII) versus the more practical-based IFS with the business owners who were sending their staff on the course.

He asked them: "If you've got someone who's qualified, would you still send them out to see your best clients?" and they said, "No. We would never put our young graduates on their own in front of our most senior clients because you still need credibility. They still need experience – at least a couple of years".

As Darren explained: "It's the same as a junior doctor, junior solicitor, Paralegal. It's the same principle."

He told me that these business owners all agreed that it is important to have a great overview when training, but when you need the technical information you can obviously go and look up the technical documents, or you call your broker consultant who 'usually knows this stuff inside out'.

Darren reminded me that even the most qualified and experienced advisors still ask more experienced colleagues for help when it's a difficult case.

Darren used this information as the basis to significantly improve the results of his financial adviser school and produce qualified financial advisers who more closely matched the requirements of the Quilter business.

The qualifications are more practical, and, as Julian the current academy Director says, "*a level four is a level four -It's a national qualification of equal merit.*" One of the great things about using the LIBF is that it ends with a really in-depth case study, so it's very practical and ensures that the advisers who come out the other end are capable of giving advice rather than just academic.

Julian feels that in the old days there were too many people who just got the academic qualifications without actually having the people skills to be an adviser.

Addressing the cost of training

Previously in this book, Cameron has explained the cost and challenges of setting up as a self-employed financial adviser and Daren has explained the small number of adviser academies on offer.

Furthermore, at the time of writing, the SimplyBiz Adviser Academy has recently had its second poor OFSTED visit and questions must be asked about its viability.

So, we have looked at the old-fashioned self-employed adviser route and also the academies (where they exist), but neither really looks capable of addressing the gap on their own.

It is still one of the hidden secrets of our profession that training is expensive and is not usually fully funded. Most individuals need to find a way of supporting their living costs while training, and sometimes even their training costs while most businesses are only happy to hire fully trained and proven financial planners and advisers.

Estimates of the cost of training seems to vary. Sean McKillop estimates the figure to be £50,000-£60,000.

Someone has to pay for this training. When the Quilter Financial Adviser School was under Sesame Bankhall Group, it was designed to operate as some sort of service for the industry. Adviser businesses paid subsidised fees to train up their new advisers.

When costs became prohibitive it was sold to Intrinsic and moved to being a profit centre under Darren's tutorship.

Darren told me that previously it had been very difficult for a Financial Adviser School (FAS) to make a profit in the traditional sense by charging trainees directly, with low pass rates. When it was sold to Intrinsic, they significantly improved the pass rate and member firms were charged the training fees so it was able to turn a profit.

After Darren moved on, Julian took over.

Under Julian's direction, the profitability of the Quilter Adviser School is now gauged on longevity of service within the Group. If an adviser remains with the Quilter business or one of its subsidiaries for at least two years after graduating from the school, that's deemed as being successful and profitable for the business.

So, with a different remit, any financial adviser who remains with one of Quilter's businesses for at least two years after graduating and becoming authorised does not have to pay any training fees.

Applicants to enter the financial adviser schools

The number of places was cut back during the pandemic. In the case of Quilter, only 50 financial planners graduated fully qualified and were appointed from the financial advisor school in 2021. This compares with around 3,000 within the Quilter Group, so is still a drop in the ocean. Nevertheless, it is starting to be more successful.

So, despite all the challenges, with so few adviser school places available, there is no shortage of applicants.

At present, the majority of advisers are sponsored by one of the network members and they could be employed or self-employed within a network member business. However, the national, which is full of self-employed advisers is starting to grow, and they're starting to take a few people.

But there is good news from St James's Place on the horizon. Sean told me that one of the things he will be working on is the evolution of a paraplanner and what he calls a workplace academy -so that he can help those people, who may have an ambition to move into an advice space at some point in the future, to start some of that journey whilst they're still in their current role.

> "Well, wouldn't it be brilliant if these young people could earn while they learn and contribute what they learn, because they're already doing paraplanning jobs or admin jobs or, or whatever. That £50,000 then stops being a cost and starts being a contribution. Doesn't it?
>
> "Over the last few years, we've been able to facilitate more and more of this type of internal recruitment. So, we work with some of our bigger practices, and they join the practice in a role with a potential view to becoming an adviser at some point in the future. Some of our best results are now being achieved with that internal recruitment model."

I asked Julian about the future. He thinks that there is an ambition within the industry to build financial adviser schools and bring on young people and career changes. He also says that 32% of those going through the financial adviser school are women, which suggests we will see a gradual improvement in gender balance across the profession.

The major issues they need to overcome are:

1. The time it takes to qualify as a financial adviser;
2. The difficulty in earning an income quickly, and the lack of employed positions for trainees within the financial advice profession.

Providing a realistic route to earning for newly qualified financial advisers – earn while you learn

A big barrier to people becoming financial advisers is the lack of earnings while training.

The concept of paying people to train is still quite alien to many of these businesses, which places tremendous financial strain on those individuals choosing to train and become authorised in the hope of earning big rewards later.

As we will see in the next chapter, Cameron passed his level 4 diploma while in his previous role and it was funded by his previous employer, so he incurred no training costs.

Nevertheless, even though he was fully qualified and authorised, the current remuneration system seems to be stacked against a new person joining the profession.

For a self-employed adviser it will take a while to build up an income, and he or she can't generate any adviser income until he or she is qualified, so it's quite common to remain in another job while qualifying. I guess this is similar to a London cabby studying for the knowledge in his or her spare time. However, this does narrow the talent pool to career switchers willing and able to fund themselves.

One initiative is the 'fast-track' course for career switchers used by Quilter and St James's Place. This allows individuals to become fully qualified and able to practise within a three-month period, ideally while they're being paid elsewhere or living off their redundancy. Julian explained:

> "We built a structure that would allow firms to take somebody into their business as a trainee, so they're doing some work to help the firm whilst getting the necessary qualifications. We then took this mindset that said if we treat it like an apprenticeship -the principles are to bring somebody into the industry."

It also helped ensure that trainees could start to cover their costs more quickly. Just like Cameron Renton, financial advisers don't need to rely just on giving investment advice when starting out. Darren expanded:

> "You have them work to do that. So financial benefits to the company are that once they've got their first exam, they can start going out, writing protection business.

> "And then we incorporated CeMAP (Mortgage qualification) so that after three months they can physically start completing a few mortgage cases, so they're actually generating their own value, covering their costs.

> "So actually, in that period of time, they can also start marketing, start trying to generate business for mortgages. And that might be through referrals of clients they've been to see; they've written the protection business for. And then they've got a further six months before they get their final exams under their belt."

The network needed to have worked very closely with the IFA firms and restricted adviser firms and then go out and find this new blood.

However, in addition to that, Quilter's national business has long-standing deals with affinity groups, which generate adviser leads from referrals. These affinity groups are a legacy from previous acquisitions of Lighthouse and Charles Derby Groups, and have a full-time team working on them to generate them. These leads (particularly protection and mortgage leads) give an adviser an opportunity to earn commission relatively quickly from the non-regulated side of the business while they take longer to build up their income from wealth and assets under advice.

Retaining those who qualify

Darren turned the financial adviser school from 60 graduates per year when he took it over to 300 graduates at the end of Year 3 and a 50% graduating rate to about 95% over the same period. They also added a level 6 programme for those interested in pursuing advanced qualifications.

All three academy/school directors I spoke to freely admitted to underestimating the task of supporting and retaining their school's early graduates.

Julian is keen to stress that he and his team are learning from this and there is now far more focus on continual support for the first two years after graduation.

Julian recognises the strange situation that accountants, solicitors and doctors are employed and earning a wage while they're training, whereas the majority of financial advice firms are too small to pay salaries, and therefore, most financial advice trainees have to generate their own income in some way while learning.

He reminded me that there are exceptions. Even within the self-employed giants, some of their adviser businesses do employ people, thus ensuring they receive some payment while they learn.

Sean McKillop explained how SJP works to ensure a high retention rate.

"We teach people brilliantly. Well, we've also got to train people equally as well to apply what they've learned.

"That programme will last several months and again, needs to be funded, when you look at the programme itself, the management of it, the managers and the specialists that we bring in to support it. And the paying of the would-be partners to go through it. You will soon rack up £50,000 to £60,000 in investment, but we believe absolutely it's the right thing because if we get the selection bit right, and deliver world class training and support, we'll get a return on that investment in the years to follow.

"I think one of the biggest challenges that this business has faced in many years is the retention of the right quality of people. People don't go elsewhere if they're able to earn enough to live the lifestyle that they want to live.

"So, for me, the success of this all starts with one thing, and it's going to sound extremely basic, but it's something I think the industry has

not done brilliantly well, and we've focused a tremendous amount of time on over the last couple of years.

"And that is: your retention starts with the right selection, not recruitment, but selection. And I have a very simple delineation. If you like, recruitment means you get to the point where somebody wants to join you. Selection is the next stage for me and selection is where we choose those people who want to join us, who we wish to invite onto the programme.

"Yes. I only have a finite number of places. I will not continue to expand and expand and expand. That allows us to be selective, to make sure we've got the right people with the right drivers, motivations, behaviours, capabilities... what you will... to join the programme. There are two types of people and you distil all the way down. There are people who are joining as advisers in existing practices, and there are people who are joining to be partners, i.e. business owners in their own right. And we have different positions for the different audiences."

So, retention is high on every academy's agenda. While that will not surprise too many people, it's good to know there is a recognition that we still have a long way to go.

Training issues need to be addressed

The industry will find a way to make financial advisers profitable while they are in training. This may be by using an industry training levy (like football). We need to create an easier career path which is open to more than just the wealthy individuals who can fund themselves for months, if not years before turning a profit.

Once this is settled, employed training roles will emerge. Just like the legal and accountancy profession.

Financial advisers will be able to earn while they learn through building out the training schemes alongside the academies.

We have seen how the current reward model is, quite rightly, stacked against 'get rich quick' people and yet many of the companies offering training are still using a self-employed model which makes advisers dependent on writing new business to survive. And we have seen current adviser training academies turning out newly-qualified financial advisers who are expected to be self-employed.

I predict we will shortly see a better, more professional approach to training for new industry entrants.

Shortly, we will see how Cameron used his own money to bridge the gap and how he purchased leads and sold commission-based non-regulated policies to make ends meet. Cameron is diligent, exceptionally brave and fortunate to have the finance in place to do this.

We have seen how career changers are often expected to continue working elsewhere while studying for the diploma. We know how some newly qualified advisers find it difficult to find the clients they need to become profitable.

In my view, the widely accepted industry approach of not paying people while they are training, is a massive barrier to entry which needs to be addressed. Financial advisers need to earn while they learn. I was delighted to learn from Sean that St James's Place are taking steps to addressing this.

Both Sean and I started out as broker consultants in major insurance companies. The training was high quality and well funded and we were employed on a reasonably competitive salary while on the training scheme. Once trained we received a decent salary, great bonuses and a company car. I have no doubt that my parents would not have supported me forsaking my secure, reasonably well paid (but extremely dull) job in a bank for self-employment, so I am delighted to see a few academy places are offered by firms giving employed roles. As Benjamin Beck told me, that's the best way to widen our appeal to new entrants when we are ready to do so.

Once that becomes more widespread, it will become a proper profession designed to attract the brightest and best, and not just those who can afford to take a risk and work for nothing for a long period.

I can already see this happening on a small scale where financial advice businesses (often part of the big three mentioned earlier) supply clients and leads to help their new financial advisers start the ball rolling, but it isn't easy.

Of course, the big problem is that it takes time and experience to become an effective financial planner. Financial advisers take time to develop their skills. It takes time to build up to managing wealthier clients who tend to need very experienced advisers.

Louise Hunt admits that her newly qualified advisers are not necessarily ready to take on High Net Worth clients in a private client practice from day 1.

> "The really qualified advisors have been in their position about 20 years ago, and they had to earn their way to that position. You have to learn your trade. You just don't expect to have that kind of interaction. Because you don't have the knowledge and you don't have the experience. So, it's not like a lot of jobs where basically you're in three years, you're qualified and that's the end of your qualifications and you level out."

Young and newly-qualified financial advisers need an employer who will nurture them, but those are rare in the current market.

Louise Hunt said to me that you never stop learning.

> "It's quite a challenging environment. And it's about using your brain a lot and talking to people.

> "And you have to start as a junior and then work your way up to get that. And again, you earn respect in this world. And that's by walking the walk, instead of talking the talk. I think you have to deliver in this environment rather than just say you can."

What we really need to see is larger advice companies taking a longer-term view, bringing advisers in on employed contracts, paying them as paraplanners and administrators while they train, and then giving leads and clients when they qualify and become authorised.

These advisers will be happy to earn a reliable employed wage in exchange for looking after clients and learning their trade.

It needs a big firm to do this. Possibly some of the consolidators.

In my view, the future employment model for all but the largest product-provider-owned businesses will be employed, but very few of these companies are currently offering training contracts to new industry entrants. Instead, only the really large players are running academies and most of these expect the advisers to work on a self-employed basis once qualified.

I predict this will change. If this matter isn't sorted, I suspect the industry may have to consider funding training through an industry-wide levy, like the Government apprentice scheme.

CHAPTER 10 SUMMARY

- 56% financial advisers are expected to retire in the next 10 years.

- Almost every financial advice business wants qualified advisers, but very few are prepared to train them.

- The best funded, fastest growing companies are not prepared to wait. They provide client banks and are prepared to pay a premium to hire experienced financial advisers.

- I estimate that we need around 2000 new advisers to qualify per year but the four main academies/adviser schools combined currently train around 700.

- Barriers to entry are high but the financial advice profession has less appeal than the legal, accountancy or medical professions to university students.

- The large academies have enjoyed some success with career switchers, particularly from the military and professional sports.

- The profession is trying to reach out to minorities (both gender and ethnic) but there's more work to be done.

- Few companies offer employed roles to entry-level staff but the self-employed route does not appeal to most graduates. Companies need to find the way of helping advisers 'earn while they learn'.

CHAPTER 11

New employment models

All new industries go through phases as they grow. Tracing the role of the financial adviser from the 1960s through to the 2020s we've seen a steadily changing role. In the early days, financial advice was like the wild west. The earliest settlers relied on prospecting to find clients for the new products and the concept of caveat emptor (let the buyer beware) was the order of the day.

Since then, we have seen increased professionalisation and regulation. No longer is it acceptable for someone to be a milkman on a Friday and a sharp-suited financial adviser on a Monday. There is no doubt that the early prospectors did a lot to get the industry going and innovators such as Lord Weinberg came up with innovative solutions. These behaviours were largely driven by commission. It could be argued that some people became very rich at the expense of their clients.

Through each iteration, we've seen greater regulation and more consumer protection. From the Financial Services Act 1986 onwards, caveat emptor has been overturned in favour of consumer protection and it's hard to conclude this is anything other than a good thing.

This professionalisation has, however, led to an increase in the value of financial advice businesses as income has become more measurable and certain.

The financial services industry has become more corporate, seeking protection in numbers. Most would argue it's almost impossible now to follow the traditional entrepreneur's route to market by setting up a one-person financial advice business, as the ability to quickly make some money from a small group of clients has largely bitten the dust.

It has also led to significant reduction in new people entering the industry, as we have yet to develop a suitable alternative which hires at a rate fast enough to replace those leaving the profession.

The traditional approach

To understand how much has changed, it is helpful to look at an example.

- Before RDR, a financial adviser with no experience and minimal qualifications but good prospecting skills might be capable of selling two savings plans per week, which might easily pay £1000+ per week in commission from a standing start.
- As he/she became more experienced, he/she might add investment bonds and pension transfers to his/her offering.
- When RDR was introduced, the same financial adviser selling two savings plans per week would only earn around 3% of the amount invested – which might equate to £72. Not surprisingly, advisers stopped selling savings plans!

So, the idea of setting up a business and earning quickly by advising an individual with few savings was well and truly over!

Under the old commission system, it was possible to earn a reasonable living from a few new business cases, but the downside was that the salesperson sometimes didn't understand what he/she was selling and therefore may not be advising the client well. He/she was only as good as his/her last sale which might place unreasonable pressures on him/her to make the sale at any price.

In more recent years, companies began a long, slow transition towards ongoing fees.

Initially, and well before RDR, we started to see a small amount of trail commission on investment bonds (perhaps 0.25%) in addition to the traditional initial commission, but as the industry moved towards fees and away from initial commission, we started to see many adviser businesses adopt a model which looks more familiar today, with 0.75% to 1% ongoing adviser fees most common.

Let me give you an example. Cameron Renton is one of the new generations of financial planners, but he has followed the traditional self-employed route to become an IFA. It hasn't been easy.

He is aged 38 and recently moved from being a BDM at Prudential with a basic salary, benefits and bonus to a self-employed IFA role, working in a cost-sharing arrangement with a sole practitioner IFA in Scotland. He found it really difficult to make the move to financial planner even though he had the qualifications already. He spoke to many financial advisers who were not willing to take on a trainee, even a self-employed one, until he eventually found one.

"One of the challenges for a lot of people is that if you'd already fully qualified, there aren't that many options out there for you. Academies wouldn't take me because I was already qualified and other employers or other advisers are not necessarily willing to take you on because they have not got the size and scalability to do that.

"I was a BDM earning about £40,000- 45,000 a year, but I had £10,000 in savings. And I decided to take a leap of faith to go across the divide, to become an adviser. I'm really fortunate. I've found a senior adviser in the Edinburgh area who I have got a real good relationship with.. We effectively run two separate businesses from the same premises, however he takes regulatory responsibility for both businesses. . The plan is I will eventually take his business over, but for all intents and purposes, I am responsible for me. So I have effectively gone from having a £45,000 per year basic salary to having no salary and no clients. I've got a wife, I've got three kids, I've got a mortgage. I have passed up big bucks to make this thing work for us."

Cameron has entered with his eyes open.

"Whilst it may be tough for five, six months, actually, the long-term potential of the role, given that we've got an industry that's got a lot of people retired and not many people coming in means there is going to plenty of work for me.

"I'm working alongside an adviser who is in his early sixties and looking to potentially retire in the next two or three years. That gives me plenty of time to learn from him and get the basics."

Cameron is not typical but has managed to move from one part of the industry to another. That is a big challenge because the gap between a self-employed financial adviser's starting income and that of a BDM, technician or even a sales support is significant.

It is a big financial challenge which Cameron does not underestimate.

"It is still quite a drop in salary and it's not everybody who's prepared to take a significant drop in their income. I have a bare minimum need to cover my half of household expenditure, etc. My wife works full time with a bank. So, she's got relatively decent earnings, but to cover our overheads I need a modest amount of money a month. So, I look at it and I need to do a minimum of two or three protection pieces of business in a month; I need to do a minimum of one decent investment case plus a piece of protection business. But I also have to understand that it doesn't work in that fashion."

I asked Cameron why he didn't take an employed adviser role? He said employed roles are very rare. Big companies only seem to want young graduates. Also, big companies tend to have restricted offerings and he wants to be an independent adviser.

In an industry where the companies are mainly very small, and most don't have the resources to offer on-the-job training:

*"You have to find a potential employer. Of course, that has to be a larger business. Doesn't it? There are only around five thousand adviser businesses and hardly any big enough to hire **and** train me."*

He is right, of course. There are only around 50 large financial adviser businesses with over 50 financial planners and a further 500 or so scattered throughout the UK with between 6 and 50 financial advisers. He is fortunate to have found an adviser who will mentor him, but he doesn't underestimate how difficult this is for an ambitious person wanting to start out as a financial adviser.

"The difficulty for a lot of adviser firms is, if you're one of these one-man bands, you're probably making a really good living yourself, but you're not prepared to take a £20 or 30,000-pound hit in your salary to bring somebody into the business. While you're probably quite happy to mentor some young financial advisers, they haven't necessarily got the ability to just hand over a client bank as well."

As a lot of financial advisers used to do, Cameron has to find his own clients. He buys leads from 'unbiased' and others but it's a risk. He explained:

"I've taken some leads from them. To give you an idea, though, I've had about 45 inquiries from them since I signed up about a month and a half ago, and I've got four clients from it, but yet again, the vast majority of them I have ignored because they don't match my advice proposition. So basically, from unbiased you receive certain leads and you choose which ones to buy.

"The way it works is that I register my preferred postcodes. I've got my home address, which is in a suburb of Edinburgh and people can search either based on the offering that they're looking for, say a pension within five miles of their home address. And it ranks you based on your destination."

To build his client bank he chooses to be less discerning than others. While others set minimum investment criteria, he does not.

"I've actually found that I've been picking loads of people up in that £10,000-£20,000 bracket. Now, whilst it's not big-ticket stuff, once I pay my fees to the network and all the bits and bobs, I'll maybe clear £600 quid out of it. It's another client on my book; it's another half a per cent ongoing. It's another bit of our assets under management.

And it's another piece of experience for me as well, you know, and that's the way I look at it."

It will take a long time to build up the ongoing advice fees by just relying on these small investments.

One of the attractions of becoming a financial adviser is the ongoing financial adviser fees, but to earn £50,000 ongoing adviser fees, Cameron knows he will need to secure at least £10M in client assets under advice and so he aims to supplement these small investments with a few wealthier clients!

Cameron is also willing to work anti-social hours.

"I've got people on my client banks who are night workers: they don't work a nine to five shift. They are working first in the morning till last thing at night, or they're working on night shift. So, I actually see them before they go to the shift, 8 o'clock at night works for them, or after a shift, 7am. As a new financial adviser coming into the industry, I think you have to be able to embrace it. You have to be open; you can't come in with a closed mind."

Cameron has really taken the traditional (some would say old-fashioned) route into the financial advice industry. He has embraced the opportunities he sees and has made light of the challenges.

But to do this he has gained his qualifications while being employed elsewhere and then given up a well-paid job and fallen back on savings to fund himself and his business while building up clients and income. He is happy to take on clients who others would consider to be unprofitable and is happy to work unsociable hours where the client requires it.

I think Cameron's story gives us a really good explanation of the difficulty the financial planning profession has in attracting new advisers. The majority of businesses are subscale and do not have the clients or infrastructure to support the training of the next generation of advisers.

As nearly 90% of financial advice businesses employed five financial planners or fewer and while they may have some spare clients, they'll probably find it difficult to justify the cost of bringing on and training a new financial planner. At a rough cost of £6,500 to train someone to level four standard plus the cost of salary while they're training, it's not a small amount and there's a significant risk that the financial planner will leave at the end of the process, tempted away by a higher financial package from a big company.

At the same time, of course the larger players in the industry have a vested interest in training their own. They tend to own client banks and have the scale to employ individuals while they train them.

We have an industry where there is a shortage of qualified advisers but also one which is full of small firms who do not have the scale and capability to train their own, with a compensation model geared to businesses that already have strong revenues and client banks.

Just like in the accountancy and legal professions, where unqualified and part-qualified accountants and solicitors in large practices do a lot of the work, part-qualified advisers can still make a contribution to a larger financial planning company by providing support or even paraplanning for others to sign off. However, the number of academy places compared to the needs of the industry presents a big gap.

One of the best and most suitable sources for financial planners is people who already hold the qualifications, but currently work in another part of the industry. However, as Cameron learned, big companies only appeared to want young graduates.

A more mature candidate will probably find themselves joining a business on a self-employed basis, having to carry their own expenses and find their own clients. At best they can expect some mentoring from the supportive sole practitioner, IFA or similar with the view to buying their business out at a future date. The cut in earnings will make this very difficult. Individuals need to be willing to take that cut.

There is definitely a place for this. Julian Hince told me that their mature entrants often work in other industries while they are gaining their professional qualifications. Quilter has a team dedicated to keeping in contact with these people until they pass their exams and then bringing them into some of their adviser practices at the point when they are ready and legally able to advise clients. This contrasts with other professions such as accountancy and legal, where trainees only qualify after they have worked in the industry for a while.

Benjamin Beck now runs FAM, a community which supports new people wanting to join the financial advice profession. He is well aware of the challenges new advisers need to overcome.

He told me that the first challenge is to secure an academy place, and that is not easy for someone with no experience. Secondly you need to work incredibly hard, longer than normal hours, to qualify. Then you have to get your qualifications and then your competent adviser status (CAS) within the firm.

But he was keen to remind me that that is only the start of the challenge. The hardest part, in his view, is to develop the soft skills and secure some clients.

> "Everyone wants to know the formula and yes, it isn't easy, but it's about giving, starting with one client, giving them a good service, earning the referral, and onwards. And that's a lot of the work I've been doing."

He thinks self-employment is a step too far for most.

> "I know many people have no choice but to accept a self-employed adviser role in order to get into the profession, but I know it puts most people off. Personally, I'm a single man without any dependants, but I still have bills to pay, and with the market as it is and client acquisition being tough, I would not go self-employed myself. I'm grateful to be in an employed role. If you look at the profession as a whole, in order to get more people joining it I hope there is capacity out there for more firms to offer employed roles because if you have to consider self-employed, and you have your commitments, you are unlikely to do it."

Ben stresses that it goes against the whole concept of putting the client first.

"When you have that safety, you can focus on doing a good job and having a good output. Whereas if you don't have that financial security, you start panicking -and that's when you don't do a good job for people because you're focused more on bringing in the money as opposed to providing a good output".

Ben's view is that forcing someone to start out self-employed is dangerous: "Because you're focused more on your needs than their needs."

He is not afraid to make sacrifices, however.

"It might be necessary for earnings to go backwards before going forwards. A trainee financial adviser may choose to accept a pay cut while training in order to make progress. I remember a call with a candidate who was on a reasonable salary and looking to move to an administrative role, and wanted to ask me about the pay differences. And it was quite significant. But then again, if you are ambitious and driven, there is no reason why, for instance, you can't surpass the administrator's earnings later on once you qualify and build up your clients. If you are good at client acquisition, you'll get back up there. I'm not saying it's easy. It's not at all easy, but it's... it's possible. Others have done it. So can you."

Of course, it's not all bad news. The academies have been a success to some extent, particularly where companies own their own clients. But we still have some way to go before we are able to replace financial planners at the rate they're currently leaving the industry.

Cameron's approach is to be commended and he will, no doubt, reap his just rewards over time. In many ways, he is taking the well-trodden path of many entrepreneurs. But, this model, as we have seen, has its limitations and, as we have seen from Terry Ellis earlier, the financial advice profession with its high barriers to entry and strong regulatory approach is no longer attractive to many entrepreneurs, and may be more suited to detail people who are more process-driven.

The employed financial planner model

Although the employed model has been around a long time, it took RDR to really get it the traction necessary to become the main way of working for many.

Before RDR, the most common users of employed financial planners were the retail banks and the professional practice-based businesses such as accountancy firms. As they had a ready source of leads, they didn't need to pay the high rewards needed to encourage entrepreneurial prospectors of the type the rest of the market required. Instead, the focus was on professional salaried advisers who focused on client work.

By paying an attractive basic salary and motivating bank staff to provide leads, the banks realised they could keep a higher proportion of the commission they earned because advisers spent less time on prospecting and more time advising clients, thus generating a higher level of fees per adviser. Back before RDR, HBOS was known for the fact that commission generated for the bank per financial adviser was 6 times their earnings, i.e., their earnings were 17.5% of commission income. This compared with a typical employed financial adviser earning 33% and a self-employed adviser earning 80% of the commission they generated.

So, employed advisers are inherently more profitable for adviser businesses although their fixed costs will affect capital adequacy.

However, that's not the only reason that employed advisers are more attractive to many ambitious adviser businesses.

For any business owners looking to scale, they will need to bring in other financial advisers to look after their clients.

The relationship between the clients and the advisers is crucial.

In most cases, a self-employed adviser will own the clients they look after. As a result, when looking to sell an adviser business, only the income brought in by employed financial advisers has a value.

The employed model is the most effective and profitable model for a typical financial adviser business. However, it is also the most expensive to set up due to the fixed overheads and, importantly, it challenges the capital adequacy requirements.

Business Value Employed v Self-Employed Financial Advisers

Example 1 all employed	Example 2 all self-employed
Financial advice business. All financial advisers are employed.	Financial advice business. All financial advisers are self-employed.
1 principal and two employed advisers. £100M AUA £50M advised by principal £50m advised by employed financial advisers £1M income £500K EBITDA	1 principal and two self-employed advisers. £100M AUA £50M advised by principal £50M advised by self-employed financial advisers £1M income £500K from the principal Deduct all income associated with the self-employed financial advisers (£500K) Net income £500K Recalculated EBITDA £150K
Estimated Value (@ 7 x EBITDA) c **£3.5M**	Value (@ 7 x EBITDA) **£1.05M** (reduction of £2.45M)

So, with the smart money backing the employed model, we can look at the model in detail.

Once we moved through RDR, profitable businesses moved their focus from selling savings plans to managing assets. Suddenly client books had an ongoing value and the type of financial adviser needed moved from sales to advice.

This is by far the most common model used by medium and larger companies, and with the entry of PE firms to the sector, it's where they see the value of the businesses they are funding.

Ambitious, scalable business owners now separate the advisers from the clients. They use multiple touch points with people to ensure a client feels like he or she is a client of the firm and not just a client of their financial adviser.

They tend to use M&A to purchase client banks and other adviser businesses and then bring in high quality financial planners to advise and grow the client banks and associated ongoing adviser fees.

By contrast, the traditional adviser businesses are less able to take multiple income streams from products, platforms and funds so they are more reliant on advice fees than the large product provider and asset-manager-owned financial adviser businesses.

As they grow – and some are seeking to make money from added services such as will writing, mortgage advice, in-house fund management and investment platforms – they still need to make allowances for overheads and profit from the financial advice fees.

With the employed model, the key to profitably in deploying a financial planner is to allocate leads or clients to them which can generate income quickly to cover their salary costs. As the business will have devoted time and money to building up its lead sources and/or client bank, it will be anxious to maximise profit from them and also to ensure retention if an adviser leaves.

New self-employed model – generating income fast

The traditional self-employed financial adviser who generates his/her own clients is becoming less profitable and less attractive to new industry entrants who may consider the time taken to become successful through this route no longer justifies the input required.

The traditional financial advice network model relies on small businesses to band together for shared services such as regulation and compliance while individual businesses and self-employed financial advisers keep the majority of their fee after network costs.

Unfortunately, the largest 50 financial planning firms lost £1M each in the recent FCA figures. The only part of the industry which lost money. We can deduce one of two things from this.

Either the networks are retaining too small a part of the income to be profitable, i.e., their costs are too high, and their retained income is too low -so the self-employed model is suiting the self-employed advisers but not the businesses they work through who carry the risk and regulatory responsibility.

Or

These financial results don't show the full picture, i.e., a larger parent business is making money from other aspects of the financial advice business (for instance fund management) which is not shown in the accounts of the financial planning business. They are investing for the future, anticipating more profits 'down the line'.

I suggest it is a mix of both.

Some of the traditional networks are struggling for profitability due to an overdependence on founder members who draw too much.

On the other hand, we know, for instance, that many large companies see their adviser businesses as distributors of their products and that is how they make their money.

In a corporate world where volume-related bonuses are frowned on, this can be sidestepped if the financial adviser is considered to be self-employed.

The product provider or asset manager parent company's principal way of making money is through their other fees, so they can afford to be generous to their advisers, often allowing them to keep the majority of their adviser fee in the knowledge that they the provider or company is making money from other parts of the service.

We have also seen the mighty Prudential (whose advisers now work under the M&G brand) also attempt to introduce a new self-employed model for its advisers who work through a wholly owned subsidiary. This new model supplies leads and clients owned by the parent company to its advisers which ensures they can reach profitable income levels much more quickly than Cameron's route above. It is not the first time Prudential has reinvented its financial distribution model. I will look on with interest.

A traditional financial advisory practice business owner will be interested in building profit but also capital value from the business as they might sell it one day. A product provider or asset management business, however, might just regard its financial advisers as distributors of funds -in which case, the main interest will be in funds generated and it may have no interest in building capital value through the advisers, seeing them as a trading expense, not an asset.

Often, the product provider's focus might be on capital adequacy, preferring to keep the financial advisers as 'cost of sales' rather than an ongoing business expense, which probably explains why Prudential and St James's Place both use the self-employed model to ensure less strain on capital.

Even then though, the self-employed model on client ownership varies. SJP locks customers into its products through exit penalties but gives the advisers ownership of clients, whereas Prudential clients can exit but Prudential owns the client relationship and presumably views the self-employed financial advisers as merely 'client handlers'.

While St James's Place has nominally self-employed sole proprietor businesses under its wing, even these businesses are growing their employed adviser numbers as larger businesses buy up the client banks of their retiring partner colleagues. And of course, the partner practices, and not the employed financial advisers, own the client relationships in this case.

The next generation of large businesses are the Corporates. They are able to make money from vertical integration by taking money at all stages of the food chain. Not just from the advice fees but also from platform, custody and investment management fees. They may be happy to cross-subsidise these losses in the short term, but they are keen to retain their clients.

For them, it might be argued, financial advisers are crucial as a means of distributing their products but not necessarily expected to be a source of profit in their own right. This appears to be causing the large product providers to look at the fastest way to scale their financial adviser teams who can ensure client acquisition and retention.

So, we may see a new type of self-employed adviser arise. One who is rewarded for his or her efforts but can become profitable more quickly than the traditional model as clients are supplied by, and continue to be owned by someone else.

The traditional self-employed adviser model for small and medium financial advice businesses will die out over time

As we have seen, the current self-employed model is no longer fit for purpose for any business aiming to build value. While the sole traders may continue, offering a limited range of services to a small group of clients, self-employed financial advisers within larger business are value detractors for any business owner wishing to sell.

Some of the largest financial advice businesses are networks whose members are smaller self-employed adviser businesses. Even before the pandemic, the average top 50 financial planner businesses lost £1M in the previous financial year (FCA figures). Some of these have attempted to share the pain with their members. In particular, some are often not yet mature enough to support the business with ongoing income alone. These businesses suffered during the lockdown and the advisers will have suffered. These networks also have little value compared to those advice businesses where the financial advisers are employed, and the clients are owned by the business.

Of course, some of these businesses are making most of their money from other parts of the advice chain (platform, investment and custody fees) so things are not always what they seem. Some networks charge lower fee retentions to financial advisers who place client assets on the company's in-house investment platform. Nevertheless, some of the networks are struggling to change their model into one which is profitable, and I believe the change from self-employed to employed will continue for all adviser businesses not owned by product providers.

I expect the self-employed model to die out over time for all but the smallest owner-managed sole-trader businesses.

The remaining self-employed model will be for big product provider businesses only

However, the one exception is the large product provider-controlled adviser businesses (currently St James's Place and Quilter but soon to be joined by M&G). These seem committed to it and may continue to have a 'controlled' self-employed financial adviser model if tax authorities allow it.

Their interest is in keeping liabilities and capital adequacy costs low, using their self-employed advisers to service their clients while retaining ownership or control of the end retail clients who invest in their products and services, while making money from associated parts of the value chain.

Although each of these three businesses has a self-employed adviser channel, Quilter also has a small employed adviser team in its private client business. Both Quilter and M&G also distribute products and services through the intermediary channel.

However, each has a different approach to client retention.

St James's Place only has one direct sales channel. Their retention method is to lock in the clients. Even though SJP financial advisers are described as owning their clients, they cannot leave the business easily with their clients. It uses exit penalties to retain clients, meaning it is difficult for clients to move their assets to a different provider.

Prudential 'owns' its clients and advisers cannot take them away. Its recent purchase of an IFA business also means the company's most successful financial advisers who may want to become IFAs can do so without leaving the Group. This is likely to help client retention.

Quilter operates across a wide field. Financial advisers in the network own their own clients and could move them away. Instead, the business owners are incentivised to stay for economic reasons through support services. They own their clients and can choose to move them away.

In recent times, Quilter has been keen to focus on profitable financial advisers, purposely shedding those who it deems to be unprofitable, focusing its resources on those who can manage larger, more profitable clients and generate new client assets for them.

CHAPTER 11 SUMMARY

- The employed adviser model is becoming more common for growing advice firms with financial backing.

- These firms often acquire other adviser firms and client banks, employing highly productive financial advisers which significantly increases the value of the firm.

- Traditional firms, using a self-employed adviser model will find that, should they wish to sell their firm, they have fewer potential buyers and therefore a lower value due to concerns over client retention.

- The pace and cost of client acquisition means that setting out to be a self-employed adviser is a step too far for many.

- The traditional self-employed model will die out over time for small and medium financial advice businesses.

- The large product providers such as Quilter and Prudential (now part of M&G) are re-building direct salesforces, using the self-employed financial adviser model. They see financial advisers as routes to market or distributors and this approach needs less capital.

- Financial adviser fees are relatively unimportant to them and can be paid to the advisers. They can make money in the rest of the value chain.

- This new type of self-employed financial adviser doesn't own their clients – they merely 'look after' the clients while they are with the company.

- The big companies all use different methods to ensure client retention and keep their financial advisers loyal.

CHAPTER 12

Processes and working methods

As we move into the future, financial advice will continue to be delivered in a greater variety of ways. Technology will support the advice process to ensure financial advisers are used more efficiently and the income generated per adviser rises.

While interest rates are just starting to rise, we anticipate a low interest environment for a while to come. This creates a greater need to drive efficiencies and costs will come under increased scrutiny.

Any part of the value chain which can be commoditised will be. An example of this is the investment platforms where, despite significant re-platforming costs and investment, there has been a lot of consolidation as the players seek even greater economies of scale.

Just like in retail, the distributor with scale and the closest links to the client is able to take control of the value chain.

It is in this environment that the value of adviser businesses has begun to rise.

Technology

The COVID-19 pandemic has undoubtedly been a game-changer for many people. There is no doubt we are in the middle of a digital revolution whether we like it or not and it's amazing how quickly the UK was able to adapt to home working and keep functioning when lockdown took place.

COVID has given the world a real chance to appraise the value of digitalisation and its effectiveness in a real-life situation. Too often in life, we start trials in unrealistic circumstances. Whereas in the case of COVID-19, the lockdown -in Britain and across the world -has meant technology, such as Zoom and Teams, could be tried in real-world situations where people had no choice. These technological solutions have undoubtedly been a winner, and now virtual meetings seem here to stay.

However, it's not as simple as that. Although most home working worked OK, many of the large product providers with big, centralised operations struggled to adapt initially as many were dependent on PCs (rather than laptops) linked to servers. Furthermore, firewalls were often in place to stop remote-based staff from accessing the 'mainframe'. However, by the end, most of these issues were overcome and many companies, looking at the costs savings which could be made, have at least considered home working.

From the financial planning perspective, we know that financial advice businesses are mainly small and flexible so, not surprisingly, they have adapted pretty well to video and digital technology.

Many of us were already familiar with Zoom, but I didn't think that we would be relying on it on a daily basis back as recently as early 2020. Zoom's daily active users jumped from 10 million to over 200 million in just 3 months at the start of the pandemic. Zoom and Microsoft teams both struggled initially, but within a relatively short time everyone was used to it and many of the early glitches had been addressed.

Recently, I tried for the first time to have a video call (via Zoom) with my cousin in Alice Springs, Australia. The experience wasn't altogether satisfactory; it proved impossible for us to run the video and listen at the same time. In the end, my cousin had to turn off his video to get a stronger voice call.

Even locally, one of my retained clients tried to brief my head of research and I via Zoom, for a senior C-suite role. He was at his home just outside London, but he might as well have been in New Delhi. In the end, he had to abandon use of the video to get a basic signal strong enough to talk to both of us.

Even when reception has been clearer, there's no doubt it still has several problems in a business context, where what is said and the way it's said can be crucial. And if there is a dispute, who can prove what was due to hearing and memory and what was caused by technology?

Digitalisation and technology will undoubtedly affect the world as far as financial advisers are concerned. Well before lockdown, there was a general fear that the older generation (who account for a large part of private client wealth in this country) wouldn't cope with virtual meetings. On the whole, my clients tell me that it's gone well. They've been able to get their points across, backed up by documents, and by post or email.

Client relationships have persevered and, if anything, many older clients have adapted more quickly to video communication and online reviews than might have been anticipated at the start of the pandemic.

The client experience and how advice is delivered

The biggest question wealth management and financial planning businesses still need to address going forward is whether they will continue to embrace technology and how and whether they can engage new clients for a complex service via video technology.

Can we truly advise people in a manner with which they are happy? Surveys indicate that people want options including digital, face to face, and using technology such as conference calls and video technology where required.

COVID-19 accelerated our move to technology but did not necessarily fundamentally change the way financial advice is delivered. Of course, the need to communicate is human and older people have adapted out of necessity to stay in contact with family members they could not meet face to face.

Recent industry studies such as one by Boring Money in May 2021 say 49% of clients were happy to receive advice via video (+24% from 2020). While older clients still prefer face to face, the view of video technology as a means of delivering advice is changing quickly.

Financial advisers did not suffer income loss as was feared they might. Many of the World's stock markets fully recovered all their losses from COVID within 12 months – and as many advisers' ongoing adviser fees are based on assets under management or advice, it means their income recovered too!

However, while reviews and ongoing adviser fees carried on largely as normal, many reported bigger impact on their new business as it became harder for their financial advisers to add new clients during the pandemic.

This was not universal feedback, but I have received anecdotal suggestions that the younger keener advisers adapted faster than their longer-standing older counterparts.

It has made us all evaluate our lives and the unnecessary trips we make, the time spent in the car visiting clients when we could just jump on a Zoom call.

Many people I speak to are looking at the cost savings that can be made by not meeting face to face, but I think we need to be careful of commoditisation. All businesses can re-evaluate what part of their financial planning service can be delivered digitally. Beyond this, advice businesses would be wise to share cost savings with clients and not use them as an excuse to increase profits.

According to Boring Money, 40% of investors would favour paying a lower fee for digital advice while 29% said they would prefer face-to-face advice even if it would mean higher fees.

For many, the key will be to segment service properly, digitalising some back-office functions but providing high value additions such as human intervention at key points in the process to preserve margins.

A few years ago British Airways ran a clever commercial where an American businessman had a video call with a salesman and his team in the UK. This was in the post 9/11 era when companies cut back on flying and video calls were becoming popular.

The two sides had clearly been discussing a deal and the American ended the conversation by reassuring the UK team. He said he was happy with the deal and would check and sign the paperwork later that day. Both sides ended the call.

The scene cut to the UK. The team congratulated each other on a job well done and deal about to be signed.

Then the scene cut back to the American in his office. His assistant showed a rival, apparently far eastern, delegation into his office and he welcomed them with a smile and handshakes all around. The message was clear, flying across the world to meet face to face gives you a greater chance of winning the deal compared to a video call!

Nowadays, in the world of e-signatures and screen sharing, matters have improved slightly but for many, the casual introduction will be more difficult. It will give the holding supplier, whether that is an adviser or other vendor, the opportunity to lock in a relationship and lock out the competition. This will just make relationship building harder.

A personal observation from our recruitment business is that virtual interviews make it easier for interviews to take place but harder for hiring managers and candidates to make a personal connection. We have noticed that it is much easier for an employer to counter-offer candidates who have never met their potential boss in person, and also that home-based employees hired during the Covid period feel less loyalty to their employer and are more likely to move on quickly. New clients will be harder to secure so it will be even more important to put time and effort into maximising the value of relationships with existing clients.

While most financial advisers are currently oversubscribed, this situation will not last forever.

As the Author Daniel Priestley recently said:

> "You do not want to become commoditised. You do not want to enter any race to the bottom... Lowering prices and taking products online is a fast track to commoditisation and it's something you should be particularly careful of doing."

It has let us all sit back a little and think about what is important to us and how we do things.

Digital technology will supplement but not replace face-to-face calls where it is economic to do so.

There is still a great desire for face-to-face interaction although a blended model will become more common.

However, there will be growth in low-cost models to close the advice gap. Digital solutions will be used to provide limited financial advice models for those who can't afford full service financial advice.

Digital transactional financial advice will be a natural extension of call centre type arrangements, such as those used by Hargreaves Lansdown and others.

However, many of these financial advisers will use a mixture of video and telephone technology and not be overly dependent on where they work, so the traditional 'office factory' will be replaced by flexible working, partly from home and partly from the office.

Is this the beginning of the end for urbanisation?

Back in the 19th century, the industrial revolution led to people flocking from the countryside into the towns to work in the new machine-powered factories. However, even though the factory workers lived in the towns and cities, often ending up living in appalling conditions, the factory owners quite quickly moved out of the cities away from the smoke and became the first commuters.

Move forward to the late 20th century and commuting had become quite an unpleasant experience with many professionals squeezing into overcrowded trains that run late or were cancelled.

No wonder we saw the rise of the urban professionals.

First of all, Dockland living became popular, London docks and others were upgraded and modernised. More recently we've seen conversions of many office blocks into residential living and people have been quite happy to move back to trendy apartments in the centre of cities. We shouldn't have been surprised. This has happened in cities like New York and Tokyo for many years. We've certainly seen a big uptick in urbanisation in the early 21st century.

It now looks like a COVID lockdown may have caused people to question this. When the lockdown came, many young urban professionals found themselves living in areas where coronavirus transmission was very high. London, in particular, had a very early spike as people living on top of each other infected each other very quickly. London, as one of the most connected cities in the world also proved to have no defences to prevent the virus being brought in from abroad.

Subsequently, with people restricted in their activities and many people working from home or even furloughed, people in the centre of cities found it impossible to socially distance themselves.

By contrast, COVID numbers in the rural areas, in the south-west of England, rural parts of Scotland, Wales and Northern Ireland, have remained lower. This is largely due to proximity. People live farther away from each other, and it is much easier to socially distance. Certainly, I'm fortunate enough to live in the countryside and it was evident that we have double benefits of gardens and plenty of space to exercise in.

Not surprisingly, this has caused people to reconsider the attraction of living in a city. Also, working from home has been tested and many people find they like it.

At the time of writing, house prices in the predominantly rural south-west are rising much faster than they are in the cities.

Large companies will move out of their expensive city centre offices

There are also various surveys out there which talk about whether advisers will close offices or not.

My opinion is that we undoubtedly have to change to the digital world, but there's no one size that fits all.

Whereas large companies focused on profit margins see the whole pandemic as a great experiment and the chance to cut offices and cut costs, this won't necessarily be the same across all sectors.

There is a real chance that improvements in 4G and 5G technology will mean the centralised way of working, still used by many large companies, will no longer be seen as vital. Instead, we might see the rise of more local hubs, where people value the benefit of working in teams, while they avoid the high cost of city centre rents.

Company head offices will be smaller and will be used partly as meeting hubs. They will house fewer staff who are just there to keep the building ticking over and be on hand for visitors.

I noticed this trend with my own IT support company. Whereas they all used to operate from one office fairly locally, they are now adopting a one-week-in-five schedule where a couple of the staff work from the office to enable clients to pick up and drop off computers and other tech needing repair or spare parts, while the majority of the team provide client support direct to their computer while working from home.

While many of the staff value the sociability and interaction in the office, many don't. From a personal perspective I have found those in training and those who are doing the management and training need to be in the office while others may not.

Our own offices, based in North Somerset, in a country house, could well be the way forward, acting as a hub. Staff can be home- or office-based or hybrid, depending on their role, while benefitting from the human interaction, with the office offering a great meeting place for clients.

Increased hub working

Whereas 30 years ago, it was the case that the life insurance salesman came to your house (to close the deal). Increasingly, financial advisers and wealth managers have set themselves up as professionals encouraging clients to visit them at their offices, during office hours (9AM to 5PM), as part of this attempt to be recognised as a profession.

I believe this will continue for many of the regional and professional practice connected firms. Advisers know that presenting the right face as the business is important to clients who are investing considerable sums of money with them.

The value of financial advice, on a face-to-face basis and as a personal service, is not to be underestimated. Many of the regional firms have known this for years, choosing to operate from small, easily accessible offices, up and down the country.

Car parking has often been a prerequisite, so their clients can visit them and their offices as well, of course, as advisers visiting the clients at their homes.

While many older IFAs are happy to work from home, many young people appear to value the social interaction and training support available from working in an office with others. There is considerable benefit to mental health as humans are social beings. What has become apparent is that many of the businesses, at this point, believe there's considerable value in asking the clients to come to their offices.

In my experience, wealth manager and financial planning businesses are fairly equally distributed across the country. And many of them choose to have modern office premises based outside of town centre -for practical reasons, e.g. parking is usually easier in the suburbs. Also, in business parks.

When I look out of my window at the trees and wildlife, which includes squirrels, rabbits, birds of prey and other wild and domestic life, I really wouldn't want to be back in the concrete jungles of my youth.

We've seen practical examples of how very large companies can work with a skeleton staff, providing the technology is good enough. Where technology has fallen down, it's often because we hadn't anticipated the type of working required.

From what I've seen of many large company business plans, their disaster plans were based on damage to their main office with a back-up central location. When the pandemic happened, every location was affected. I predict that there will fewer and smaller city centre offices and people will be more reluctant to be involved in long commutes, with an increase of small work hubs allowing flexible working. Many people will divide their time between home-working and the office.

The demise of the company car!

Despite the fact that people use less public transport, we're also going to see much less travel in general. With advisers being able to mix between various digital technologies, I think the annual review meeting will become even more important, but that otherwise many advisers won't need to travel every day. Company cars are likely to become a thing of the past.

Years ago, the large product providers all provided company cars to staff and it was seen as a major perk. Over time the government has attempted to tax this out of existence, and we see the big increase in the car allowance which, when added to a higher figure for fuel claims could more than offset the benefit of a car after allowing for tax.

Looking forward, it is harder to see how car ownership will be justified in the same way. The move to electric vehicles means a car's capital cost may remain high but the travel cost will be low. This model will more than justify the future self-drive Uber or equivalent where advisers can order a car to the door on the day they require it, drive or allow the car to self-drive to the client, returning home and sending the car back to the Uber centre.

Using Virtual Reality (VR) in training

This may sound futuristic but virtual reality in training is already happening. Sean McKillop explained to me how St. James's Place has invested heavily in this to help trainee advisers learn from virtual roleplays. By developing a variety of VR training programmes, they have been able to extend the reach of their academy from four physical centres in London, Solihull, Manchester and Edinburgh to others based further afield.

> "They'll go through this comprehensive training where we use a blended approach. Virtual reality then is a driver. But, with as much done face to face, as we can. COVID was actually what drove me to make that decision.

> "I removed a geographical impediment. It's not great if you're stuck out in Norfolk, or Exeter so we have created a universal academy which is no longer constrained by geography and that wouldn't have been possible without the advent of some of the technology solutions that were ultimately driven by what COVID made us do."

In Sean's view, it ensures that the academy lives and breathes in all the SJP locations around the country and all the partner practices are recruiting because they can deliver VR training directly into those practices.

People learn best when they're surrounded by other people, so they can learn at their local offices, surrounded by successful partners and advisers, and most importantly their local managers are able to answer any question they have.

Use of technology

Terry Lawson worked as a financial planner for two of our retail banks for many years before moving into a professional practice IFA business. By 2017 he said he had fallen out of love with the industry due to regulation and paperwork. He now works as a senior business development manager, selling software solutions to IFA businesses. He told me that he loves his job.

At the time of our meeting, he was working for Synaptic Systems, a leading UK provider of software solutions.

> "I sort of fell out of love with the industry, so I can sympathise when I'm talking to an adviser or a network or... or a provider or an investment manager. I understand the issues our buyers are facing now with MiFID to PROD and the need for complete transparency."

Now he feels the software his company has developed helped advisers.

> "So, whilst I'm selling the software and the tools that we have, I'm looking after a bank of clients, providers, networks, and I'm able to go and have these conversations with our development teams. I can say, "we're developing this now. This is what it needs to do". I'm in a position where I can make a difference because I can talk to our developers."

He explained to me how a typical financial advice business has digitised in the past few years.

> "When I worked for HSBC, the business world was very much paper-based.

> "Today, if an adviser or paraplanner uses our entire suite, they've got everything there that they need when they're giving advice to clients.

So, they'll do a pension transfer. If they use any cashflow analysis, that's there. If they want to do protection research, we've got that too. Attitude to Risk (ATR), risk planning, risk profiling. We can do that for them.

"So as an adviser, if you're giving a client advice on whatever aspect it might be, we provide the research tools that will feed into the IFAs' back office system. For instance, if they use an IO back office system (one of the market leaders) , our software and our solutions will feed into IO."

I asked him for an example.

"If an adviser is looking to give Mr and Mrs. Smith some advice on their pension planning, they can come to us, they can use our research. It might be a product research or fund research to make sure that they've got the accurate funds that they're looking at for the risk category. They will assess the attitude to risk through our risk profiling tools.

"They might want to model the investment journey. So, our model or tool will give them that illustration, e.g. "if you invest this much money every month from now until 15 years away, and we're taking this view on your risk, we're using this kind of asset allocation, it will give this much at the end.

"We licensed the Moody's model. We can use the Stochastic Modeling to show what those outcomes are going to look like. We can also show them potentially what the downsides are. Capacity for loss is a big thing, so it really helps advisers who use our questionnaires with their client."

You have technology when you start today, but when Terry was a financial adviser it was more paper based. He did have a corporate fact-find and admits that being paper based made the customer feel comfortable, but it was very labour intensive.

Modern technology has made the job much better as far as Terry is concerned.

"If I had modern software back then, I may still be advising now because it makes the job easier and more enjoyable. It gets the client even more engaged. And when you're having conversations about investment, risk and capacity for loss, that engagement is just critical, so trying to build in everything that we do on our software helps the client fully understand."

Terry thinks the best thing about technology is the ability to send something to someone that can then be opened and completed on their phone, then sent back, all in a few minutes.

"An adviser who deals in mortgage and protection advice for example, they've got their own website. We have a very, very easy tool that they can embed into a website. It means if you want to go and get quotes for life cover on their website, you can simply put your basic details in.

"The first screen is 'I want level term insurance'– name, date of birth, occupation. If you're looking at something income protection wise, the next screen is the amount of cover you want; the term, critical illness. Yes, no, that kind of stuff. Click the button for the quote and the quote's there in front of them.

"They can't apply for it because it's designed only to generate the lead. Whereas the majority of life insurance companies out there involve you filling your details, then maybe three, four screens of information... click for a quote... and then it says someone will be in touch. With our tool they will "have the quote, a number illustration there and then, and the key facts. It will tell them if these people are cool, a number to give a call to. It'll also then send me an email to say, 'Joe Bloggs' has just done this quote. Here it is. It's already put that into my web line licence for me. So, I just had to go into my web line and all the quotes on there or the details. I can have a really good warm chat with the clients. I've got their email address, their phone number, so that's pretty cool as well.

"Technology can never replace that interaction that you have with people by sitting in front of them and using a pen and paper."

Robo advice

Finally, increased efficiency through technology might have the dual benefit of helping companies deal with the shortage of financial planners and offer the use of artificial intelligence (AI) for the less affluent for simple transactional advice work.

Today we already see glimpses of AI technology all over from driverless cars to drone trucks delivering groceries, so it's not too much of a stretch to see the current quote requests being extended to guided advice and beyond. At present, the regulatory regime discourages execution only and may not allow complete AI advice, insisting that an authorised financial adviser will still have to sign it off, but that may change in future.

What will the technology-driven millennials want? Like a lot of parents, Terry has strong views.

> Of course there's a big generation coming through. This generation where everything is on handheld technology. Their heads are down all the time as they're glued to that little screen in their hand. That's what they want, and to an extent they no longer have the ability to communicate in the real-life way we do now. This is a generation where communication skills have deteriorated, but in a way evolved too, to a level that would suit something like robo and AI advice.

So financial advice will need to adjust for 'push button' millennials.

Decentralisation and global relocation of many functions

As the process is segmented, it becomes more evident that the financial adviser's face-to-face skills may be the only part of the process which requires someone to be based locally.

Functions such as paraplanning and other office-based functions will move out of city centres and back to the home, but later, will relocate across the globe to places where there's a high supply of highly skilled staff prepared to work at lower salaries.

Paraplanning is undoubtedly highly technical, and we've seen a significant rise in the chartered paraplanner. These people have a lot to offer, but as many know, this can be done from home.

On the whole, the paraplanner is not heavily involved in conversations with the client. While the hybrid paraplanner/adviser support person may well speak to the client, there are many paraplanners who do not have any face-to-face or verbal interaction with clients.

Any role which doesn't require verbal or face-to-face interaction with a client can be carried out from anywhere in the world with good communications and broadband. There are parts of the World such as India where a highly skilled postgraduate can be hired much more cheaply than in many western countries. Offshoring is not just an industrial phenomenon. We're likely to see it apply to paraplanning, administration and other back-office roles.

In an increasingly global world, where a UK-based chartered paraplanner might fetch a salary of up to £60,000 per year, they need to focus on personal interaction if they wish to stay ahead of commoditisation.

CHAPTER 12 SUMMARY

- Financial advisers are taking control of the value chain.

- The global pandemic sped up the move to video meetings. It worked well for client reviews, but has been less successful in new business.

- Most people want options from face-to-face to video and online digital.

- Digital will supplement but not replace face-to-face calls where it's economic to do so.

- There will be growth in low-cost models to close the advice gap. Robo advice and use of AI will rise for millennials but those who can afford a full service will still appreciate an element of face-to-face.

- We may see a reverse in urbanisation with a focus on local hubs outside of city centre.

- Company cars will become a thing of the past.

- Companies are already experimenting with virtual reality in training which increases the size of the talent pool.

- Technology is being used by advisers within the advice process but advisers use face-to-face contact for key interactions with the client.

- Those not in the face-to-face part of the financial advice business should be concerned about relocation of their job across the world to lower cost, high-skill economies.

CHAPTER 13

Mergers and acquisitions – the rising value of an adviser business

Financial advice businesses had almost no value until quite recently, and now they have the potential to make their owners millionaires overnight.

Whereas in the past, a financial adviser might just close his or her business on retirement, because it had little or no value, this has now changed.

RDR, the end of commission and the replacement by fees created ongoing revenue streams for financial advice businesses, and a consequence is that businesses now have ongoing value, and a market in buying and selling financial planning has grown up.

In the 'old' commission days, advisers only made money from clients every time a transaction was required (and this sometimes encouraged some pretty ropey practices). IFAs can now make money from their businesses quite literally in their sleep.

Most financial adviser practices conduct periodic reviews of clients' investments and undertake the occasional overhaul. However, many are paid their fees based on client assets under management which is withdrawn from clients' assets on a monthly basis. While this suits most clients because it's a small, regular payment which they feel they don't have to pay personally from their bank account, it also suits most IFAs as it means ongoing income.

The practice buy-out

The first people to recognise the value of adviser businesses were the product providers. The direct salesforces, including Abbey Life, Allied Dunbar and St James's Place introduced the practice buy-out, offering advisers a capital event on retirement. This was partly a recruitment move as it helped the direct salesforces attract established advisers to transfer their clients to the company, but it was also a defensive move as it ensured policy retention.

The client bank once purchased, could be sold onto another member business, thus ensuring the clients were retained and serviced rather than lost to an IFA who would, no doubt, move the clients, over time, to other companies.

This model has been remarkably successful. There is a considerable internal market for client banks at St James's Place and many networks followed the same approach. It is almost self-funding. The parent company effectively transfers the clients from one partner/member firm to another and funds the purchase by lending money to acquiring partner firm, who repay through the ongoing fees by authorising the parent company to withhold them as they are withdrawn straight from the funds.

Using the St James's Place model, as the practice buy-out amount payable is a multiple of ongoing fees (possibly 6 x plus a 25% premium), the interest and capital can be repaid from the ongoing fee income that the clients pay and the new partner makes money from selling more new products to the client, gaining referrals and other income.

By the time the acquiring partner retires, the debt will have been repaid and they have an asset to sell onwards. St James's Place has effectively established an internal market for ongoing client retention and adviser acquisition.

Here's an example.

A SJP partner wants to retire and exercise his, or her, practice buy-out (PBO).

They have £30M assets under advice (invested in St James's Place products). And this generates £150,000 per annum in ongoing adviser fees (0.5%). The PBO pays £150,000 x 6 = £900,000 plus a 25% premium (£225,000). The individual exercises the PBO and receives £1.125M.

Another partner buys the practice and SJP funds the deal. The new partner repays the PBO from the ongoing adviser's fees of £150,000pa and he or she makes money from the clients through new investments and referrals. When the new adviser retires, their loan will have already been fully repaid and they will be able to use a PBO from SJP to buy them out (maybe for £2.30M).

The outgoing partner is happy as he/she received £1.125M. The acquiring partner is happy because he/she used the client bank to build his client book and now sold it for £2.30M. St James's Place is happy as it has retained the client assets on which it charges fees for fund management, platform and product costs.

The market for buying and selling IFA businesses

Where the product-provider-owned sales teams had led the way, the IFA market followed. The market for buying and selling IFA businesses was established.

Once RDR occurred, the barriers to entry were established. Financial advisers now needed a level 4 financial planning qualification such as DipPFS and also needed to charge fees. With typical wealth fees of 0.5% to 1% of assets, £10M AUA was required even to create a modest turnover of £50,000 to £100,000 pa ongoing, so for those without wealthy connections it became almost impossible for someone to build a business from a zero start. While there are exceptions (such as Cameron), many found it necessary to buy a small client bank in order to get started. Acquisition was becoming an attractive route to market.

While the market for a St James's Place partner practice is restricted to other SJP practices, the IFA businesses, and even restricted businesses with a wider choice of offerings have a wider appeal.

When a financial adviser is ready to sell his or her business there are many companies keen to buy, recognising the ongoing value of the client relationships he/she has.

After a shaky start for IFAs, when early adopter companies such as Towry Law often overestimated the value of self-employed adviser businesses, or, in the case of Bellpenny, failed to integrate clients into their business, companies gradually created an effective market for buying and selling IFA businesses and client banks.

There are many different valuation models but typical values for small IFA client banks may be three times to four times ongoing financial advice fees (OAF).

For example, for the small IFA similar in size to the SJP practice above, the fees might be £300,000 per annum (1% ongoing). The multiple might be 3.5x, giving a sale price for a client sale of £1.05M.

For larger companies, the purchasing company may be using far more complex calculations.

If the business is larger, with staff who are likely to remain after the takeover, the payment is more likely to be based on a multiple of ongoing profit. This is often described as adjusted EBITDA -earnings before interest tax, depreciation and amortisation, adjusted to allow for any increase or reduction in ongoing costs expected after the sale.

While the usual multiples seen for mid-sized businesses are 5-7 times adjusted EBITDA, some can be higher. The really large financial advice businesses are aiming to build and eventually sell for 10-15 times adjusted EBITDA (or more) and there are exceptions where for very large businesses, the multiples are much higher still.

Consolidation

No one size fits all but consolidation is the direction of travel. Firms will continue to merge as many retiring business owners take advantage of market conditions to 'sell up'. And those who remain in the market, look to scale.

Small and sole adviser businesses are the core of the market. 89% of the financial advice firms market employ 5 or fewer advisers. Most will remain small until they reach a point when a director is looking to exit. At that point, many sell up or merge with bigger competitors to fund the exiting director.

The medium-sized regional businesses (The next 10%) employ 6-49 advisers. Regionals tend to be in a decent position, having a long and trusted position in a local community and often less reliance on new business income. Most are reasonably profitable but struggle to grow organically so the ambitious ones will need to grow through acquisition. They have adapted well on the whole, although profitability can be an issue, and needs to be worked on before sale or merger terms become attractive.

The top 50 adviser firms (1%) employ almost 50% of the total financial advisers in the market but they are not a homogenous group.

As groups grow and merge, the small sole traders will drop away. Currently, 31% of financial advisers work for advice firms with 5 or fewer advisers and many are sole traders. In the end, I believe that over 95% of advisers will work for firms with at least five financial advisers.

Large and medium vertically integrated advice businesses (often owned by a product provider or investment manager) have a plan and will stick to it. They tend to align the acquisition of clients with the hiring of additional advisers. In the case of director earn-outs, the transition can be managed through timely recruitment of financial planners to take over the client bank.

The challenge of organic growth means larger businesses are focusing on buying competitors and client assets under advice. As an industry we are already seeing many sole and small advice businesses selling up to the large consolidators or regional firms.

In a defensive move, some of the large product providers are already making a move for the small advice business owners willing to sell to them to ensure they don't lose supporters, and their clients to vertically integrated firms who will move the client assets away.

The Private Equity (PE) companies enter the market

The resilience shown by the financial planning sector during the COVID pandemic was not lost on the private equity companies keen to spot the next great opportunity. They have entered in big numbers, driving up M&A activity and deal values.

Compared to a few years ago, financial advice businesses have ongoing income and for many of the more mature businesses, this alone will have been enough to see them through the worst before markets recovered. Financial Advisers did not hide away during COVID. They spent time supporting and reassuring their clients and most were rewarded by a recovering stock market. The Financial Advice profession weathered the storm very well indeed.

While the greatest challenge to the industry, is undoubtedly a shortage of financial advisers, this can't be turned around in an instant, just like it takes a number of years to address a shortage of doctors, teachers or other professionals. That means demand for financial advice is expected to exceed supply for some time to come, presenting great opportunities for well-funded ambitious advice firms.

Of course, it could be argued, the shortage of financial advisers may take even longer to address. Whereas a single employer in a state-dominated industry like schools or the NHS has the HM Government, with its deep pockets to fund recruitment, a group of competing financial planning business owners may be less likely to cooperate with a one size fits all solution across the profession.

We will need to come to terms with the reducing financial adviser numbers, increased digitalisation and the opportunities and threats that creates.

This PE money is seeking a home for 5-7 years and sees the financial advice sector as offering attractive low risk returns. We've already seen a massive move to consolidation. In the current market, where many existing players are trying to grow and new entrants are using PE money or Debt funding to get into the market, we know there is a wall of money waiting for someone wanting to sell their profitable and successful financial planning business.

At present, I'm seeing a number of financial adviser businesses in the 2-10 adviser bracket seeking to grow but often being surprised at the competition they face, and prices being paid when trying to acquire. They have often sacrificed profitability to grow but almost without fail they have shown ambition to grow but haven't quite realised how fast the market is moving and the access to capital funding required to achieve it.

Author of the entrepreneur revolution and other business books, Daniel Priestley says that companies that are most vulnerable have between 13 and 50 employees, which is the stage when they start needing a larger infrastructure which adds cost and dilutes profitability, but then, once you have cracked that, companies can make 'super profits' which go with being a professional firm.

One of the acquisition directors from a major consolidator recently said to me that he believes there will be two stages for consolidators.

Stage one – buy and build (5-7 years). From launch to first capital event This means just buying a group of advice businesses and leaving them to run independently with little central interference for a period while benefiting from a valuation purely based on scale (leading to increased EBITDA multiples) until sale or re-finance.

Stage two – integrate and consolidate (5-12 years). Start to integrate the businesses, centralising costs where possible and driving up profitability for a second sale or refinancing.

It may seem counter-intuitive not to drive economies of scale in the first five years, but he insisted it is the fastest way to make money in a rising market -just like a property speculator buying a small number of 'doer-upper' properties and just selling them on in a rising market, leaving the next buyer to do the hard work. Of course, there are many different approaches and recently I have noticed several acquirers are using business model and culture as a differentiator.

This once-in-a-generation opportunity for advisers who paid little or nothing for their clients but can make a serious amount of money for selling their business will probably last the next 5-7 years until, as all markets do, it rights itself creating a balance between supply of financial advice and demand for it.

RDR has created a unique opportunity for the first generation of post-RDR IFAs to make a significant capital sum. The ongoing fees model means that client banks finally have a true value, which allows them to be bought and sold.

I say this is a unique opportunity because it is happening now, and it probably will not happen again until the next generation of Financial Advisers start to retire and that may be 20 years away.

CHAPTER 13 SUMMARY

- The value of financial adviser businesses has risen rapidly in the last few years. Ongoing adviser fee model means IFAs can now make money in their sleep.

- The direct sales businesses were first to see the value to them of a practice buy-out. By enabling one member of direct salesforce to buy another ensured that the clients remained with the product provider.

- Once St. James's Place developed their OAF model, they significantly increased the value of a practice buy-out and helped fund it, thus creating a value for a partner exiting the market.

- Where the direct sales teams led the way, the IFA market followed. The IFA market for buying, selling IFA businesses was established. Smaller businesses are typically traded on a multiple of ongoing adviser fees and larger business are traded on a multiple of adjusted EBITDA.

- In recent years, the private equity firms have paid an increasing amount of attention to financial advice firms whose profitability was well maintained during and after the pandemic.

- PE houses typically refinance or sell their acquisition every five to seven years which means they tend to be decisive and quick in their actions, demonstrating ambitions to grow in a market which is still dominated by very small players. 1% of the financial advice firms in the market employ 50% of the financial advisers. For growth firms backed by PE or other funding we are seeing a two-part build process:
  - Part one/stage one - buy and build;
  - Part two/stage two - integrate and consolidate.

- There is currently a unique opportunity for the first generation of post-RDR business owners to make a significant capital sum.

CHAPTER 14

Summary

To truly understand any profession, it's necessary to know about its past and how it got here. In this book, I've looked at UK financial planning, initially going back to the Victorian era, explaining its origins before looking at the heady days of the 1980s, where it arguably reached its peak with 300,000 financial planners in the UK.

Back in those days, it was a sales-driven industry with a high reward culture. Focus was arguably on advisers earning the most money. I've looked at many of the practices, which help the industry grow so much, but ultimately led to its near demise. While it might be initially likened to the 'Wild West' with no regulation and a buyer-beware mentality, that wasn't going to last.

And from the Financial Services Act of 1986 through to the Retail Distribution Review of 2013, we saw a 90% drop in the number of financial planners as regulation gradually chased the unskilled, untrained out of the market. I have given a nod to the four direct sales companies on which the industry was built and explained how and why the sales reward culture came about before following the journey through polarisation, which led to growth in the independent intermediary and latterly to depolarisation, which caused the product providers to once again establish their own sales distribution channels (albeit not quite in the same mould as the original direct sales businesses).

We've looked at the rise of insurance intermediary and the latter rise and (rapid) fall of bancassurance and the reasons why. In the lead up to RDR, we knew things would be bad, but I think many people hoped there would be a way of things working out. I've tracked the lead up to the retail distribution review and ultimately the arrival and impact of it, which led to the industry's near collapse. Having seen a 90% reduction in numbers already, we saw a further 25% reduction in IFAs, and a 40% reduction in Bancassurance advisers within a three-month period after the RDR. Many thought the industry could never recover.

All things find their level and this industry proved its resilience as a small core of 25,000 financial advisers hung on for dear life and eventually found a way through by copying a very unlikely company who many had previously loved to hate. I guess when your backs are against the wall, survival instincts kick in and principles are overridden.

Since that bottoming out in 2013, I've talked about how the industry has recovered and the profession has come of age. We've now reached the stage where there's more demand for financial advice than there is supply. All advisers are busy, and most are highly profitable. Of course, the business model has had to change, and the recovery has taken some time, but I think it can now be argued that we are in the golden age of financial planning. The financial advisers of old have been replaced by highly professional, client-focused individuals who really care about their clients.

So, this is an environment where the industry can thrive, but it has many challenges to overcome. Barriers to entry are high for advisers and capital required is also high for business owners.

One of the most important issues to overcome is the demographic within the current talent pool. The majority of advisers are in their fifties or sixties (and even seventies). This of course follows a 35-year decline in the number of advisers in the market and no real appetite to grow the profession. We now face a situation where we need to grow the profession, but we're still seeing an exodus, anticipating around three-fifths of all advisers to exit in the next 10 years as they reach their own retirement age.

There are the challenges of bringing new talent into the market and training the next generation. Although the leading four advice schools train around

700 new financial planners every year, we anticipate a yearly need for at least 2000 new financial planners just to stand still. Not without challenge when the routes into the profession are not straightforward. Historically, most advisers either came through the direct sales companies on a self-employed basis or through bancassurance. The old routes no longer work.

The reward structure within this industry no longer makes a self-employed route attractive to most, and bancassurers are yet to rebuild, having downsized or closed back in 2012. Quite frankly, many recognise the need for new employment models, but most seem to think it is "someone else's responsibility". They haven't yet embraced them.

I have looked closely at the current employment models (both employed and self-employed) and their reasons for existing. At present, the majority of ambitious adviser businesses are focused on the employed route, while the large product provider companies are favouring self-employed. However, both of these models have their shortcomings when it comes to bringing in new talent.

Talking to the few new industry entrants I could find, most believe both routes are relatively unattractive and unlikely to appeal to the majority of students who want a job which pays a reasonable wage from the outset in exchange for the hard work put in to pass the required exams. Perhaps the one area which still works is career switchers who have money behind them, having already earned well in a previous profession, such as the armed forces or professional sport and now recognise the need to invest their own money in their future career development.

Many of the people I spoke to have given me clear explanations as to the challenges they want to overcome and how they'll overcome them.

For the large players who are running the financial adviser schools/academies, they're currently keeping their numbers small, but, arguably, they need to because their employment model isn't well suited to new entrants. On the other hand, the majority of businesses who are focused on an employed model either lack the funding or have too short-term a focus to develop their own routes to market, preferring to poach fully qualified, experienced advisers from their opponents. As a head-hunter,

I'm not going to complain about this, but we need to recognise this is only a relatively short-term solution.

To survive in the future, we must embrace digitalisation. And whilst there is an increase in AI/robo-advice offerings, most people seem to feel that financial advice needs to be given in person. We also have to make efficiency savings behind the scenes. There is a benefit of globalisation and the opportunities to outsource back-office services, including administration paraplanning, to offshore markets. This will all be possible and (in some cases) desirable. But again, it may damage the talent pool and the ability to develop new financial planners.

In the short term, while some of the big companies still employ a lot of people in the UK, Sean McKillop highlighted how companies are ignoring their own back-office staff as potential future advisers. And that's something we can look at.

Finally, I looked at the rising value of adviser businesses. At last, after 35 years, the value of financial advice business is rising significantly. People are recognising that the ongoing revenue now generated by a financial planning business can make it attractive to anyone investing for a return. And that includes the private equity backers who are keen to invest in adviser firms. The increase in capital funding (both equity and debt) to people wanting to build financial planning businesses through acquisition has created a bit of a feeding frenzy.

Suddenly, financial planning business owners are finding businesses could now make them potential millionaires on their retirement. Many have taken up these opportunities by selling off client banks or businesses and this is increasing the demand for good financial planners as the vendor business owners are leaving the market (and most of them are authorised financial planners).

The market for buying and selling businesses has risen rapidly from its early days of the practice buy-out with the large direct salesforces to the current PE-backed acquisitions of consolidators. While there are many different consolidation models, the one thing they have in common is that the majority have relatively short-time scales (five to seven years) in which to build and find a way for their backers to exit again. This is great for the market currently, as there's more money coming in and the current group of business owners can make more money than has been available for at least a generation and may not be available again for at least another generation. However, a word of warning, there are always winners and losers in any investment bubble.

We are in a fantastic position, as far as the public are concerned. While there is an advice gap, it will give adviser businesses time to earn higher than normal profits for a period.

In a strong market, the clients benefit too. When their financial adviser retires or dies, they won't be abandoned as happened in the past but will be acquired, either as part of a client bank sale or a business sale and looked after and nurtured by the acquiring business.

The adviser owner with a short-term view can see this as a way of enhancing their exit value while selling to a longer-term investor.

The adviser businesses with an eye on the long term can reinvest these profits in systems and improving efficiencies. They will also be in a strong position to drive efficiencies from acquisitions of competitor businesses and client banks they acquire from owners who choose to exit the market.

The best financial advisers will embrace digitalisation but not be a slave to it.

At present we have a shortage of financial advice provision, which we call the Advice Gap: the gap between the amount of advice required, and the amount of advice supplied.

But we have ambitious new businesses looking to grow and acquire others and plenty of PE and venture capital firms looking to back companies with growth plans. It's still the case that the majority of financial planning businesses are very small and specialist. They rely heavily on personal service, and I don't think that's going to change anytime soon.

Nevertheless, by that time, the financial planning landscape will look very different.

I expect to see a significant growth in the number of 'modern' large firms using an employed model and the end of sub-scale firms and a considerable curtailment in networks as we know them.

The new networks will be much more profitable using a service provider model, charging for their services and encouraging small sub-scale firms to 'sell up' or combine forces with others in a similar position. They will also add to their range of services, almost certainly adding fund solutions (even if it is outsourced).

We are also seeing some of the large product providers trying to grow without extensive capital requirements by offering a new self-employed model. This involves the self-employed financial adviser being more of a 'hired hand' than an entrepreneur, not owning the clients but taking a large part of the adviser fee for looking after them, while the parent makes most of its margin from the same client elsewhere in the value chain.

And finally – a few words of caution

If you have read this book right through, you will have noted that I have highlighted the financial planning profession's history through the early years and the dark times of RDR which eventually led to its redemption. We have seen the industry with all its strengths and weaknesses, and now, it seems like it faces a great opportunity. But I can't finish without adding a word of caution.

The attraction of the steady income streams available to financial advice businesses is drawing the attention of some people with very different mindsets to those who work in the businesses they are investing in.

While we may believe there is no place for selfish entrepreneurs in the financial advice of the future, many of those private equity backers and venture capitalists are viewing it like a typical land-grab.

As someone who has watched this evolve over the past few years, I have already seen both sides of this coin.

I have seen a number of the new generation of PE backers and like any market, their understanding of what they are investing in varies. I have personally spoken to directors of private equity firms who have invested in firms and later exited, taking a considerable loss. They have told me how they didn't appreciate the challenges of owning a business in such a tightly regulated market, and they have vowed "never again".

Some investors may have an oversimplified understanding of regulation, compliance and risk which can often be a key determinant in a business's rate of growth.

In this next part of the revolution, we will see winners and losers, and like most business revolutions, as we recognise the changing from entrepreneurial businesses to professional structured businesses, we will ultimately see it all comes down to processes and people. The priority for the financial planning profession must be to continue to keep client interests at its heart. However, the market does not stand still for long.

Watch this space. It's going to be quite a ride!

Stay updated

I hope you've enjoyed reading this book. I have certainly enjoyed writing it.

The research process, which has taken almost two years, involved talking to a lot of different financial services industry professionals and hearing their opinions.

As well as reminiscing, some of my interviews have given me the opportunity to reflect on where the industry has come from and identify the pivot points which has made the profession what it is today – as well as helping me project where it will be tomorrow and in the longer term.

I often write thought pieces and contribute to debates on the industry over on my LinkedIn. If you'd like to read them, or see what I'm up to, give me a follow: linkedin.com/in/paulharpersearch

I also regularly hold LinkedIn Live sessions discussing current topics within financial services. You can stay up to date on when these are on my LinkedIn.

If you would like a call to discuss any of the matters in my book further, or would like to share your opinion, please feel free to email me on paulh@paulharpersearch.co.uk

I speak to industry thought leaders on a daily basis and always appreciate anyone who is able to share their insight with me.

If you'd like to learn more about my business, Paul Harper Search, head over to our website for more information, including access to salary surveys, industry insights, blog posts and scorecards. There's something there for everyone.

www.paulharpersearch.co.uk

CHAPTER 15

Paul's personal journey

So that's it. I've told you about the financial advice profession. How it grew up from a group of life assurance salesman to the highly regulated profession it is today, and who would argue it's not better for the client? However, what have I been doing in the meantime?

Well, after a couple of years at the Locum Group I experienced the tough side of venture capital when I had the ignominy of being called into the Chairman's office and being asked to resign on the spot! It's not particularly pleasant, but that is the rules of the game with venture capital backers. So just a couple of years after my first redundancy I found myself out on the street again, wondering what I'd do next. Being in a relatively good financial position (insurance companies pay good redundancy packages) I decided to take the plunge in working for myself.

Initially I was offered the opportunity to set up a Bristol office for a well-known financial services headhunter. I hired a couple of consultants and learned a lot in that first year. We had a great year as a team, but our relationship with the Business Owners in London was far from perfect, and for reasons I don't wish to discuss here, I left the business a year later.

By then I knew what I wanted to do. I liked Financial Services head hunting. It played to my strengths. I could talk to people I liked in the industry I liked on a daily basis, and I could help companies to secure top talent across the industry. In the previous 12 months I'd learned the basis of running a successful head hunt business (my first year had been very profitable despite the fact that we fell out with the owners), and I knew how to hire people to work with me. On the 7th of July 1999, Paul Harper Search & Selection opened its doors. At the time, it was just me, Peter Hawkes, an experienced general recruiter taken from Reed, and Kate Allchorne, a family friend. We wanted to do things different and from day one we focused on working for clients to find top talent.

I'm very grateful for many of the people who've helped me along the way. It's always interesting when you cross the threshold to see who will help you and who won't. In the eyes of my ex-colleagues, I was clearly someone who understood the financial services profession and would clearly recognise top talent when I saw it, but of course some may have quite rightly felt that I was unproven as a headhunter. Some took the view they could trust me to deliver on the projects they needed, and some sat back for a little while, perhaps more to observe whether I might fall flat on my face!

We grew rapidly for the first couple of years on buoyant markets and I learned a lot. However, following the terrorist attack on the World Trade Centre in New York on the 11th of September 2001, we saw a slow steady decline in our market as demand for our services dropped. It was very uncomfortable, and we learned a lot of lessons, as well as losing a lot of money. Eventually we exited our prestigious but expensive premises in central Bristol and hunkered back down to much smaller serviced offices in Clifton. We'd learned some valuable lessons and just had to start again.

Pete Hawkes was still with me, and I also brought a very high-quality researcher, called Jane Banks. Everyone else left the business. When I look back on that time, I learned some valuable lessons. Most importantly, I learned that we hadn't really built a proper business. We were just a bunch of individuals doing our own thing, and the quality of the work varied with the consultant and how busy there were. I hadn't really been on top of the service levels and when I looked back at some of the paperwork, I felt embarrassed at the quality of the work delivered by some of my less capable consultants. I also learned a valuable lesson about managing money. During the first two years, while my wife, Marie-Claire, had looked after the invoicing and paying the bills, all the financial decisions had been mine. Most hadn't taken a second glance, and this had impacted on us directly. From now on Marie-Claire was central to the business and she made all the financial decisions. I just focused on recruitment.

I also realised that I no longer wanted to offer an 'okay' service to a high number of clients. I was going to focus on offering a fantastic service to a very limited number of clients who we'd built very close relationships with. That mantra has stayed with me to this day.

Back in those days, as I've explained, financial advisers were generally underfunded. Many of them wanted to hire advisers who could bring their own clients and pay as low a basic salary as possible, or even encourage them to be self-employed. That wasn't the market for us.

We focused on working with the well-funded product providers, asset managers and others. Over the next 20 years we secured a leading position in many niches. Today, if you go to a typical Financial Advice & Wealth Management conference and look around the room, many of the directors and others that you see were put into position by us, most stay in their new role for many years and that is the best evidence I can see that our executive searches are effective. Of course, that hasn't always been the case and back in the early noughties we were still building our reputation.

One of the key lessons I learned is that quality executive search starts at the top. To be proud of our business I spent many years being personally involved in every placement we made. Even today I still act as lead search consultant on MD and other senior roles.

The secret to our success has always been our team of researchers. They proactively find the best talent for us and the consultants screen and manage the interview process. The consultants are extremely familiar with what our clients want, and the **care** taken with every assignment is evident.

Developing your own team is vital. As I've explained in this book, you need to commit to develop your own talent if you're to become a really successful business. We put our researchers through extensive training and nowadays they complete an REC qualification, which ensures they know all the legal aspects and process of recruitment while we focus internally on teaching them everything about financial services and our unique approach to headhunting. All our executive search team are home grown. I think we are unusual because we work as a team, not as a bunch of individuals. Our executive search team may share out the individual assignments, and each assignment has a named consultant, but rewards and achievements are team based. It allows the researchers to be flexible and the search consultants to **share** information in the knowledge that helping any client helps everyone. It makes us different. We **dare** to be different.

You may have spotted this in the narrative:-
WE CARE WE SHARE WE DARE

Over the last 23 years, I've spoken daily to financial services professionals, and I love it. As I mentioned in the early period of our business, we were very focused on product providers. We worked almost wholly on a retained basis for certain clients, and we helped build really successful intermediary sales teams, such as the whole team at Winterthur Life, and a significant part of the team at Legal & General, Clerical Medical, Scottish Life, Guardian 1821, NFU Mutual and others. I was contacted by the sales directors when Winterthur and L&G intermediary sales teams both won industry awards. They were keen to give us some credit. By working in partnership with these companies we felt we could make a difference and they really, really valued our help.

We survived the credit crunch in 2008/9 and by 2010 we had established a significant foothold in our retail financial services and wealth management. It was around that time that some of the product providers started to take an interest in preparing for RDR. Many were looking to bring in high quality sales management in the lead up to RDR. We placed a number of senior directors during this period and, in at least one case, we helped position the company extremely well.

In the lead-up to RDR, as I mentioned in the book, one of our key clients asked us to conduct some market research about remuneration and bonus schemes after RDR. We quickly learned most companies did not have proper plans in place, which was a shock to us and a shock to our client. A few months later when RDR was implemented, it quickly became apparent that our findings were correct. The industry seemed to be collapsing around us...

As an executive headhunter, we specialise in roles which are difficult to fill, usually where there's a shortage of supply and a high demand. In the past, as I've outlined, the financial advice sector battleground was between the product providers. They wanted to influence the advisers' choice of company, which they recommended to clients. This was generally achieved through a mixture of clever product creation (such as the 'with profit' bond), good service, competitive commission terms and strong relationship building through the intermediary sales team (generally called BDMs and national account managers).

As I've already mentioned, entertainment was a very important part of this. In the early part of my head-hunting career, a lot of the work was focused on having a very high number of business development managers who used a waterfront approach to develop relationships with as many IFAs as they could. In the case of the big companies such as Standard Life, this meant having up to 350 business development people. By the time I became a head-hunter these numbers were starting to reduce a bit and the major intermediary sales teams belonged to the likes of Standard Life and Norwich Union, who still operated a waterfront approach, dealing with all the advisors in the market.

Gradually we saw growth in the telephone account management sector as businesses began to realise, they should focus their most expensive asset (their field-based business development managers) on the larger IFAs. Increasingly IFAs banded together to get better terms from the product providers in exchange for offering volume deals. This led to the growth of national accounts (strategic accounts) teams. Companies such as Legal & General were extremely effective at this, having specialist teams dealing with large nationals, large networks, employee benefits, companies, and others. As the market became more sophisticated, we saw companies separate salesforces into protection, wealth, and employee benefits and many companies started to specialise.

In the first 10 years of the 21st century, we've started to see another change. We saw an increase in fund choice for clients. Initially the major life companies still dominated, and they started to add guest funds to their investment bonds and other products. Gradually we saw the introduction of the investment platform and what was known as open architecture products, where a much wider choice of funds could be made available to people and that really helped the investment houses. Until this point, investment houses had focused on the stockbrokers and had institutional salespeople persuading life companies to take their funds. As the market opened up, the life companies started to work in partnership with the asset managers. Attracted by the big budgets and impressive head offices, we started to see life companies and asset managers running joint training sessions for IFAs, and Life Companies even holding their sales meeting in the offices of the asset managers. I often gave recruitment training to management teams. I recall Gartmore hosting the managers meeting for the Winterthur team and presenting to the Skandia sales management team meeting in Aberdeen Asset Management's London office.

In many cases the life companies opened their book of contacts and introduced the asset managers to all their major IFAs for the price of a lunch or two. This was mainly driven by cost cutting within the product providers themselves, but, looking back, could have been a major distribution mistake. Of course, once RDR hit, we moved to a whole different level. IFAs now had a total choice of who they used, and there was no relationship of obligation between the product providers and the IFAs.

Investment platforms offering a choice of thousands of different funds, put the IFAs in control. It was amazing how quickly that relationship changed. I recall the large national account managers teams cutting back on staff very quickly. Several of these individuals came to see me and told me how the end of commission effectively ended their role.

The legendary entertainment of the public providers with trips to Lords, the Cheltenham Gold Cup and other great sporting events ended almost overnight. I remember AXA, who sponsored the FA Cup at the time, suddenly found they couldn't invite their IFAs to the FA Cup Final. They invited their staff instead!

Nowadays it seems to have changed tremendously. Provider entertainment is cut down to a minimum as have the marketing allowances that the providers used to pay to the networks and national IA groups as a sweetener. They still help fund roadshows of course but it's very different.

Of course, in the lead-up to RDR, there were still plenty of advisers around. Most IFAs' businesses didn't feel the need to use the services of perceived expensive headhunters like ourselves. Our focus, as always, was on those companies which need needed and could afford our services, which wasn't the IFA businesses.

What about the IFA market?

I mentioned that before 9/11 most of our consultants worked as individuals. We had a couple who specialised in financial advisers and, as I said, their main focus had to be on financial advisers who could bring books of clients with them. We had a big success early on when we helped manage the sale of the Hymans Robertson private client business to Smith and Williamson, but on the whole, we didn't get involved in that sector of the market.

When and why did my company start to focus on Financial Adviser recruitment?

Well in 2010 we were asked to find the Head of Life sales for a leading Insurance Company. This was a direct sales company but, unlike St James's Place and many others, all its financial advisers were employed. At the time they were looking ahead to RDR and realised they needed to bring someone in who had a greater understanding of regulation than they did. Once we had succeeded by bringing in the director of employed sales from another leading player, we were asked to make a few more senior management appointments. When RDR hit, they just kept hiring.

It became apparent that RDR was a game changer. The winners were companies who owned their client relationships (or in one case controlled them). Whereas most IFAs had hunkered down, those with clients or a strong high-quality source of referrals were in a great position. A few years later, Old Mutual started to build a private client advice business through acquisition. We were ready from day one. They wanted top quality financial advisers who could take over and nurture a small bank of high-net-worth clients. This was a well-funded 'Buy and build' and we were one of two companies supporting them from day one.

Acquisitions were lined up and we were given advance notice of locations so we could confidentially approach some high-quality financial planners in advance. When the acquisition was still awaiting Change of Control, the shortlist was ready for interview. That's the secret to buy and build - timing!

Suddenly there was a small group of well-funded, ambitious, financial planning businesses paying good money and offering attractive client banks to top quality financial planners. Not all looked the same. Some were professional practice linked, some were regional firms, some were product provider backed and some were just PE-backed consolidators. Some were IFA Whole of Market, but many had a restricted offering. It's not one size fits all but they have some things in common.

- They have substantial client banks available or have an attractive lead source.
- If they supply clients, they have funds available to acquire more client banks.
- They employ their financial planners (not self-employed), and they pay competitive salaries.
- They have effective back-office systems and paraplanning support.
- They have a plan and timescales. They follow a process but hire quickly and pay well to secure the best.

Of course, then we faced the pandemic and lockdown. That has worked well for my business. A long-term competitor who I greatly respect, John Biggs, approached me just before the pandemic to say he was looking to step back and suggested we might like to consider merging our two businesses. It didn't happen the way he originally intended but in August 2020, just after the first lockdown, John and his managing recruitment partner, Charles Evans, joined Paul Harper Search, John as Chair and Charles as Partnership Director. At around the same time, we signed a deal with Martyn Laverick, a M&A specialist and long-term industry contact, which eventually led to the establishment of Paul Harper Mergers & Acquisitions. We have also brought in a number of other associates to build up the business.

Today, we see ourselves as offering a high-quality financial services talent acquisition, M&A and consulting service to an elite group of client partners. We can't work with everybody—and don't want to. We choose our clients carefully. We want to delight our clients and work closely with just a few. We can help them acquire talent and other businesses. We can provide additional services to help their senior management. We can also help business owners secure the best exit deal for themselves and their clients when the time is right.

... I work with a great bunch of extremely talented people and I am loving my job more than I have for many years!

Interviewee Profiles

Benjamin Beck

Benjamin Beck runs FAM, a community which supports new people wanting to join the financial advice profession. He joined the industry as a second careerist after six years in the British army. He joined an Openwork member firm and was trained alongside 25 other members of the openwork academy.

While studying for his diploma and receiving other training, which took 18 months, he was employed within an Openwork member firm to initially do administration and later some paraplanning, so he is well positioned to offer support to other financial advisers. He stressed that the views he gave to me were his own and do not necessarily represent the views of his current or previous employers.

Cameron Renton

Still in his late 30s and married with a young family, Cameron has risked it all to make it as a financial adviser. He explains eloquently why it is so difficult to make the transition to becoming an adviser, even for someone who already holds the level 4 qualification.

For around 50 years, most financial planners trained 'on the job' as self-employed financial advisers. However, after RDR when commission ended on investment products, most felt that the change in remuneration from high initial to ongoing adviser fees made this route nigh-on impossible. However, Cameron is flying in the face of this accepted view. He is a financial services professional who resigned from a well-paid job as a BDM at Prudential to become a self-employed financial planner.

But it's not easy, with 90% of financial planning businesses employing fewer than five qualified advisers, he couldn't find an employer who was willing to employ and train him so, seeing the barriers to entry as a positive, he has decided the risk is worth it to reach the promised land.

Cameron is following the 'traditional route' in a post-RDR setting. He is funding himself through training while working as a self-employed adviser under the authorisation of a kindly sole trader adviser and he gives a real insight into the challenges and opportunities he is facing along the way.

Darren Smith

Darren Smith has been both a self-employed and an employed financial adviser as well as a compliance professional. He saw the demise of the bancassurance model, and he was an employed financial adviser at Eagle Star which used a 'rent a rep' bancassurance model and was still there when they closed the business down.

Darren was in the heart of the industry as the vastly reduced businesses came through RDR and out of the other side, and took on the Financial Advisor School (FAS) when Intrinsic Network inherited it from Sesame Bankhall.

The financial adviser school was loss making at the time and also had a very low success rate with graduates.

While Darren doesn't claim he has all the answers to solve the advice gap and shortage in supply of financial advisers, he did ensure the school was turned from a liability to an asset for the Intrinsic group (now part of

Quilters) by improving the pass rates and getting it to break even. Many might recognise Darren's model in the various financial adviser schools we see today. He certainly has strong views on the future.

Dave Seager

Dave Seager, now an Independent Consultant, recently retired from his role as Managing Director of SIFA Professional, a specialist support organisation assisting impartial financial advisory firms to build meaningful relationships with solicitors . SIFA Professional is part of SIFA (formerly known as Solicitors for Independent Financial Advice) , where Dave was Director for 13 years. Prior to that, he spent 18 years working in intermediary sales for Scottish Mutual and Legal & General.

In 2002 there were 750 solicitor practices directly regulated in financial advice. That was 8% of the total market. Following the introduction of the Financial Services and Markets Act N2 2002, that number gradually reduced. There are now only 40 solicitor firms with directly regulated arms out of 10,600 solicitor practices in total. Despite this, the financial advice and the legal professions work closely together.

Duncan Singer

Duncan is an Aviva Manager with over 40 years' experience whose career has taken him from various parts of the South East, to the City of London, to Newcastle, Birmingham, and back round the loop again! Like me, Duncan started off his Sales career in earnest as a Life Inspector at Legal & General, following up 'green form' leads from building society managers, visiting people's house to sell them a low-cost endowment which supported a mortgage.

But when the landscape changed following the Financial Services Act in 1986, he then moved into pensions by joining Scottish Equitable (now AEGON), a leader in a new style of Money Purchase Occupational scheme designed to pick up the pieces as the UK government attempted to encourage individuals to take personal responsibility in pensions. He was involved in selling one of the only Group DC schemes on the market, a thing called a nexus pension plan, which was basically a money purchase scheme which provided a GMP guaranteed underpin.

He has also seen the reduction in intermediary sales from the heady days when the largest product providers had 350 BDMs to today when even the largest might have only 30 on the road.

Gillian Hepburn

Gillian Hepburn is UK intermediary solutions director at Schroders. She has spent over three decades in Financial Services. She is often quoted in the specialist Financial Services trade press and has risen to the top of her profession. She is also a member of the Women in Platforms group, a networking group for women in the investment platform industry.

Gillian was on Standard Life's first ever all-female graduate trainee group and is the first to admit she was fortunate to work for such an enlightened company. She first became aware of sexist attitudes when she moved into the sales division a few years later, and even then she didn't let it worry her. However, having spent three decades in close contact with IFAs, Gillian is well aware of the traditional evening work associated with the financial planning profession and said that wasn't necessarily helpful for women.

Despite considerable gender balance progress being made at board and senior level within companies such as asset managers and product providers, women only make up 17% of approved FCA individuals. This % has hardly changed since 2005.

Louise Hunt (not her real name)

Louise is a Financial Advice Manager whose main involvement with our profession has been in the post-RDR years. She moved into Bancassurance as the banks downscaled and offloaded a lot of their financial planning staff. She saw them make great efforts to put right the wrongs of the past by placing an emphasis on risk and quality of financial advice.

Later Louise moved to one of the new breed of restricted private client advice businesses which appeared in the post-RDR years.

Louise has a really positive view of the profession she has been part of for the past 12 years, explaining the changes the banks put in place to protect clients as well as giving her views on the Advice Gap and why the financial advice profession is not viewed as an attractive career choice for the younger generation of school and university leavers.

Julian Hince

Julian is the current Head of the Quilter Financial Adviser School which is part of Quilter Financial Planning.

He has worked in Financial Services for over 35 years, working with intermediaries and representing such major Asset Managers as Invesco, Gartmore and M&G where he spent almost 10 years as Investment Technical Director. He joined Quilter in 2019.

Lucian Russ

Now living in Australia, Lucian started his financial advice career in the UK as a tied adviser before becoming an IFA in London. Following emigration with his family to Australia he ran two successful advice businesses under the AMP umbrella before selling up and establishing a specialist consultancy which advises Australian financial advice business owners. He has a unique perspective.

Sean McKillop

Sean is the Director of the St James's Place Financial Adviser Academy. He is an industry veteran with 40 years' experience. He joined St James's place in 2009, progressing through regional management roles until being appointed Transition Director in 2019. He was made Academy Director in January 2021.

The St James's Place Academy was the brainchild of the late Mike Wilson. First developed just as the 2008 credit crunch started to bite. It has been relaunched in more recent years and Sean's focus is now on a mix of second careerists, graduates and internal staff development to create the next generation of financial advisers as many of the current partners reach retirement.

Sharon Mattheus

Sharon Mattheus is an award-winning Financial Planner at Lovewell Blake Financial planning in Bury St Edmunds. Brought up in South Africa, Sharon moved to the UK with her husband and young family before moving into financial services. She started as an administrator/paraplanner before taking the plunge and becoming a self-employed financial planner, working through Foster de Novo.

Sharon is passionate about financial planning, is a winner of numerous awards, and has demonstrated she can compete successfully in a male dominated profession and is modest about how she overcame challenges along the way.

Terry Ellis

Terry Ellis has been there and done it! Now retired, he was an insurance salesman and financial adviser worked in the 1970s, 1980s, 1990s and 2000s. He started with the Refuge and then Pioneer Mutual before progressing to the most famous brand of all, The Prudential. After taking a few years out to work in the family business, he returned to the World of Financial Advice at Abbey life in 1985, attending some great overseas conventions before eventually moving across the divide to become an IFA in the lead up to RDR.

He regards himself as a natural salesman who reflects on the discomfort he felt as regulation started to bite, and his view of Compliance as "the anti-sales department!".

Terry Lawson

Terry is an expert in technology provision for the financial planning profession. Having started his financial planning career at NatWest and HSBC, he spent time also as a self-employed financial adviser before changing direction in 2017, moving into the sale of software. Eventually moving into the provision of financial planning software to financial advice businesses with synaptic software, he is only too aware of how financial software can complement the personal service provided to clients by the adviser.